Ready. Set. Not)
contemplating wl.
spiritual battle for teen sexuality quite engaging. Overall, the evidence presented is strong and convincing.

—Elicia (17)

Ready. Set. Not Yet! is a life-changing book that will help shape and re-shape my generation's entire perspective on sex. It's perfect for clearing the confusing societal narrative around sex and for teaching teens, emerging young adults, and future generations about sex from a godly perspective. I believe this book will help to restore many to sexual wholeness and keep them on a positive path. I can see it being used in different kinds of discussion groups where teens can safely share their struggles and experiences.

—Jayden (19)

This is a really down-to-earth book. It explains without condemnation, and I value the apology for the older generation's silence on sexuality.

—Maya (14)

Informative, funny, and bold. An easy read, jam packed with knowledge and well organized. The imagery and visualization let you know the pure intentions of the author to connect with the reader. Everyone will learn something from *Ready. Set. Not Yet!* no matter their past or what they're presently going through.

—Makayla (18)

This is a great book for anyone struggling with dwindling morals and values because of lack of understanding and guidance about God's divine purpose for sex. I believe it will help many of my friends to get what I tried explaining to them.

—Teenage Anonymous Male

What Parents and Others Say ...

Wow, Rev. Marva, you've done it again! *Ready. Set. Not Yet!* is an incredible resource. This is the tool we've been waiting for. The next generation now has a divine opportunity to restore what is good through sexual wholeness, beyond the past legacy of shame, silence, and lack of awareness.

—Andrea Boweya, Registered Psychotherapist and Author of *Legacy Moments* and *The Heart of a Good Thing* (legacymoments.ca)

I am delighted that *Ready. Set. Not Yet!* will help millions of young people reset their minds with this essential truth: "God has chosen you in love for Himself." This book will help them to be more aware that sexual "workarounds" are a muddy distraction from the beautiful plan their Father in heaven has for their life. Enjoy the read and embrace the journey. It's not too late for anyone to recapture the timeless truths that "Auntie Marva" has so skillfully delivered to all of us.

—Chaplain Dr. Dudley Mayers (globalchaplaincycenter.com)

Submerged in the pages of *Ready. Set. Not Yet!* is the Father's love cradling many struggling young people into sexual wholeness. His gentle love will not stop wooing them. The grace fountain flowing here will help many join those in their generation who have not bowed to the perceptions and pressures of culture. This book is a prophetic announcement to present and future generations that great shall be the company of those who will relentlessly honour God's design for sex and sexuality, intrinsically re-shaping and shifting the sexual culture.

—Chaplain Rhonda McLeod, Parent and Prophetic Intercessor

Ready. Set. Not Yet! is a Bridge Builder's approach to confronting misconceptions and generational gaps in the conversation of teen sexuality. Marva has courageously shared insights, experiences, and wisdom to help prepare today's teens to stand for God's truths in the midst of adverse pressures.

—Nicola Ramitt, Parent and Bible Teacher (wordfromthetent.com)

On behalf of my pre-adolescent children, thank you for writing this book. Reading it did something to me, even as a grown adult. I realize this is what I was missing as a youth. Back then, I couldn't relate to the books I read on sexual purity because they made it seem so far out of reach. But that's not the case with *Ready. Set. Not Yet!* This book sends a very clear message that sexual wholeness is possible. As a social service professional who loves to mentor youths, I can say that *Ready. Set. Not Yet!* is the ideal discipleship resource for engaging groups of young men and women regardless of their sexual past.

—Sabrina Giscombe, Parent and Social Worker

Ready. Set. Not Yet! is a brilliant and relevant tool for a time such as this. It's a Spirit-led, practical, and easy-to-read book with a timely reminder that sexual identity, desires, and intimacy are created by God with divine purpose. In a world where feelings rule actions, with very little attention to truth or consequences, "Auntie Marva" has become a guiding light amidst the chaos and the noise. She has managed to present this subject in a way that takes the mystery and awkwardness out of conversations with the next generation about sex. I wish I'd had this resource when I was trying to figure this out on my own. I wholeheartedly recommend this book as essential reading for teens, as well as those entering and leaving the teen years. *Ready. Set. Not Yet!* is a message straight from God's heart to redeem a generation for Himself.

—Sandra Sproul, Parent and Women's Mentor

The uniqueness of *Ready. Set. Not Yet!* makes it relatable and easy to understand. The images, affirmations, and prayers draw the reader in. I'm looking forward to sharing *Ready. Set. Not Yet!* in book studies and our discipleship curriculum. The reflection and takeaway exercises are awesome because acting on what you read is a game-changer.

—Winston Campbell, Youth/Young Adults Pastor

Dianne,
Sexual wholeness
IS POSSIBLE!
"Auntie Marva"
YES IT IS
MARVA

Ready. Set. Not Yet!

SECRETS FOR TEENS ABOUT SEX

Forward by Andrew and Juli-Anne James

MARVA M. TYNDALE

Marva T. is a friend of my friend Lynne. I met her. She lives off & on – Canada & Jamaica.

One Printers Way
Altona, MB R0G 0B0
Canada

www.friesenpress.com

First Edition — 2022

End Notes contain the references for Scripture and other citations included in the book.

Contact: marva@readysetnotyet.com
Phone 416-277-6891
www.readysetnotyet.com

ISBN
978-1-03-914423-1 (Hardcover)
978-1-0.-914422-4 (Paperback)
978-1-03-914424-8 (eBook)

1. FAMILY & RELATIONSHIPS, LIFE STAGES, TEENAGERS

Distributed to the trade by The Ingram Book Company

Dedication

In loving memory of Gwendolyn Florence Houston (1937–2019).

This faithful woman of God and precious friend had no biological children. However, she was passionate about the next generation. May her legacy continually enrich youths today, and for generations to come.

Table of Contents

**The knowledge
of the secrets ...
has been given to you.**

Matthew 13:11

There's more to sex than mere skin on skin.
Sex is as much spiritual mystery as physical fact.

1 Corinthians 6:16, The Message

Acknowledgements

I'm overwhelmingly grateful to the Holy Spirit for helping me to bring *Ready. Set. Not Yet!* from concept to reality. Thank you for making me courageous in completing this phenomenal assignment the Heavenly Father entrusted to me.

Special thanks ...

To the youths who graciously reviewed the manuscript. Your responses helped to make the book so much more relevant. Above all, your encouragement kept me going to the finish line. Thanks for being such great cheerleaders.

To the parents, friends, associates, intercessors, ministry partners, and family members, including my spiritual sons and daughters. You prove undeniably that we were created to fulfill purpose and destiny in relationship. Your faithfulness expressed in so many different ways has made this book possible.

Foreword

We were teenagers when we first encountered God in a personal way. Our individual encounters with God led us to each other and to meeting "Auntie Marva." We became youth leaders, and Andrew later became a Youth and Young Adults pastor. We're now millennial parents of three young daughters, and community workers who are still deeply invested in the lives of children and youth. Through this lens, here is some of what we know to be true:

1. Entire generations have missed out on the opportunity to understand the truths about God's designs for sex and sexuality that are explained in the pages of this book.

2. This missed opportunity has created breaches in the fabric of families, communities, and cultures.

3. The repair of these breaches must start with one family at a time. As youth workers, we've always understood that it's almost impossible to out-impact a parent or guardian. What happens at home matters the most.

4. Young people are much more capable and powerful than they know.

So to the teens reading this book, understand that you have the power to bridge the gap by reaching back to your parents' and grandparents' generations and inviting open, honest, respectful conversation. More importantly, you can reach forward into your future children's and grandchildren's generations by laying the foundation to ensure that the truth is carried forward.

Invite your parents and your peers to read this book. Read it together, and start the open, healing conversations that will bring about understanding, wholeness, and restoration.

We bless you with the wisdom to understand what you read, the courage to share it, and the grace to live out God's design for your life.

—Andrew and Juli-Anne James

Founders of Streams Community Hub
Shelburne, Ontario, Canada
streamshub.com

Beloved Teen,

Thanks for checking out *Ready. Set. Not Yet!*

I've been captivated for some time now by the image of sprint athletes in the starting blocks eager for a race to begin. I couldn't think of a better metaphor for the moment-by-moment choices you have to make about sex on your teenage journey. With your body changing rapidly and new feelings surfacing, you may at times feel just like the athletes who can hardly wait to leap from the starting blocks. Sometimes you may even think that responding to the changes and feelings in your body is what life is all about. But there's so much more to the life of significance for which you were born. I want to share some of those secrets with you.

I'm so pleased that some of you have already been having open conversations with your parents about sexual matters. Kudos to you and your parents! I'm honoured to have you share the *Ready. Set. Not Yet!* conversation.

Let me introduce myself and share the backstory to this book. You can call me Auntie Marva, as some young people do. And you can think of me as a bridge builder. I'm doing my part to bridge the gap between younger and older generations, especially between young people and their parents. I'm building a bridge for your sexual wholeness. Yes, I do believe it's possible for you to honour God's design for sex and sexuality. I realize, however, that you may presently or at some point in the future need a bridge to help you cross over into the experience of that reality. I've written this book because

I also believe that a reset is always possible regardless of the situation. You can think of *Ready. Set. Not Yet!* as a spiritual GPS for the sexual aspects of your journey through the teen years. It's designed to keep you on track, but it also has a great rerouting feature should you ever need it.

I was motivated to write this book because I discovered many things about sex and sexuality late in life. Had I known them sooner, many of my choices as a teenager and young adult would have been different. No guarantees! But I do know this—what we understand from an early age matters. When we know that our bodies have a divine purpose, and realize that there's more to sex than the physical act, we're better prepared to make wise choices.

I was in my teens when I connected the dots about sex and babies. And it wasn't until much later that I came to understand that God had designed my body for purposes other than having babies. I was quite frustrated. Frankly, at times I was even angry about what the adults in my life had told me. Looking back, I desperately wished I had known some of the things that no one was willing to tell me.

I'm grateful for this privilege to help you discover the spiritual mystery about sex. It's not a small thing. It's essential for you to successfully navigate the sexual culture of this generation. During these teen years, you'll be discovering new things about yourself and trying to figure out your life. Your body will go through a major stage of sexual development, but be aware that you don't have to be controlled by those changes. I know that this book will help you overcome the sexual struggles you may already be facing or will face in the future. The secrets you discover here will help you set your heart on pursuing sexual wholeness and the great future God has for you.

One of my sons is an accomplished basketball skills trainer. I heard him say something about training his nephew that caught my attention. He said, "I'm teaching him at eleven years old what I learned much later in life—in my twenties. This way he'll be so much better at his game than I was." To you, I'll say it like this: "I'm sharing *Ready. Set. Not Yet!* with you so that you can experience a lifestyle of sexual wholeness, something that was only a dream for many in the past and even today."

Because I represent older generations, *Ready. Set. Not Yet!* is many things in one—an acknowledgment, an apology, and a gift from us to you.

An acknowledgment that it was our own fears, ignorance, and personal discomfort that often prevented us from having open, honest conversations about sexual matters. Because of this silence, you may have been left in the dark to figure it out on your own or from the culture around you.

An apology for the silence, our sketchiness, inaccuracies, and unreasonable expectations. We're so sorry! We're sorry for expecting you to follow a bunch of rules without building the right kind of relationship with you—a relationship based on truth, trust, and transparency about our own shortcomings.

A gift that will empower you to understand the spiritual mystery about sex and sexuality. It will help you to discover, sooner rather than later, the things you need to know that will motivate you to experience sex and your sexuality in God's way. It's also a gift of generational legacy that will prepare you to leave a healthy sexual inheritance for your future children.

Disclosure

It's important for you to know upfront that *Ready. Set. Not Yet!* presents a perspective on sex that may be new to you. It comes from the mind of the One who invented sex—your Creator and Heavenly Father. So don't be surprised that God's perspective is different from popular cultural views and opinions. Although not everyone agrees with what the Bible says about sex and sexuality, my goal isn't to debate or dispute these views. My mission is to introduce you to God's design—perspectives that will help you to understand the spiritual mystery about sex.

Finally, I hope you won't mind me inviting parents, mentors, and others to read *Ready. Set. Not Yet!* It's a great opportunity for us to bridge the gap I mentioned earlier. I'm sure it will bring about new levels of understanding and more helpful conversations.

My prayer is that you will come out on the other side of these pages with more wisdom, renewed hope, and clearer perspectives than you had before.

Happy reading!

Love,

Auntie Marva

What's Inside

Ready. Set. Not Yet! is a mentoring resource that invites you to interact with what you read. To help you get the most from the experience, I've divided the book into three sections with brief exercises after each chapter and section.

In Section 1 you get to put yourself in the place of champion athletes and waiting children. You'll gain new perspectives on the value of waiting through their experiences.

Section 2 gives you a sneak preview of the Creator's mind concerning sex and your sexuality. Here you'll gain an understanding of the spiritual aspects of sex and hopefully find many missing pieces of the sex puzzle.

I call Section 3 the "grace hub" of the book. It's loaded with strategies for you to access God's heart of unfailing love for you as a good Father. You'll discover the grace and wisdom you need to reach the victory line of sexual wholeness.

There's also a Bonus Section— "Find More Here." This section includes many extras, such as Sexuality Reset Prayers and a Reboot Your Mind Collection of words to live by.

Some Key Words

There are a few key words and expressions that'll be popping up throughout the book. Some may be new to you, and it's important to understand what they mean. Please take a moment to review these definitions.

Sex — Physical and non-physical sexual activities. Also, a short way for saying sexual intercourse.

Sexuality & Sexual Identity — The sexual nature of each person designed by God, including but not limited to the physical differences of being either biologically male or female. These terms also include the ability to be physically attracted to another and to be in a relationship that involves intimacy and sexual activity.

Sexual Wholeness — Your experience of God's design for sex and sexuality as His grace (favour and power) shapes your past, present, and future.

Intimacy — Being in a close, affectionate, and loving relationship that enables a person to be deeply known at a physical, mental, emotional, psychological, or spiritual level.

Passion	Having strong feelings, emotions, and desires about someone or something. Sexual passion is only one kind of passionate expression.
Workarounds	A word I've coined for the various forms of physical and virtual sexual activities that meet immediate sexual urges but deny the greater good for which God designed sexual intercourse and human sexuality. Workaround activities may range from sexting to intercourse.
Not Yet! Zone	The time God has designed to wait for marriage before getting into sexual activities.
False Start	When you engage in sexual activities before marriage (during the *Not Yet!* Zone). In athletics it simply means starting a race too early.
One Flesh Union	The biblical description of the spiritual and emotional bond that sex creates.
Soul Ties	Another way of describing the non-physical bonds formed by one flesh unions.

Getting the Most from *Ready. Set. Not Yet!*

I realize that it takes time, choice, deliberate action, and perseverance to embrace new ideas. I've included the following Chapter Reflections and Section Take-Aways to help you in the process.

Chapter Reflections

Did You Know?	A thought for you to consider.
Words to Live By	Inspirational quotes and/or Bible verses for you to speak that will strengthen your faith. The words you speak release spiritual "molecules" that build your world. These quotes and verses from each chapter are compiled in one place for easy access under the "Reboot Your Mind Collection" in the Bonus Section at the end of the book.
From Your Heart	A prayer or affirmation for you to speak that will help you get started in personalizing your thoughts from the chapter. You may also use the blank lines provided to write a prayer or reflection in your own words.

Section Take-Aways

The Main Thing	Identifies key points from the section and gives you an opportunity to evaluate how much you've embraced each truth.
Prayer Practice	Gives you the opportunity to ask your Heavenly Father to help you internalize the truths that you need to embrace more fully. This prayer practice exercise will help you grow in the habit of having conversations with God about anything. You may wish to write out your prayer. In your prayer time it would be great to also mention anyone you know who is having similar challenges.
Your Call to Action	An invitation to identify at least one specific action you're committed to taking either immediately, within twenty-four hours, or at the first opportunity. I encourage you to also use "memory tools" such as sticky notes, flash cards, or your phone to help you remember stuff that speaks to you personally.
A Blessing	Words from my heart to yours on behalf of the Heavenly Father. Words of blessing impart to you God's divine power for a safe and fulfilling journey through life.

You deserve the reward of personal growth that completing these exercises will bring about. Feel free to do them on your own, with parents, or with a mentor or a peer group. Choose what works best for you. And may I also ask you to pay it forward. Share your *Ready. Set. Not Yet!* discoveries with others in your circle.

Now let's dig in!

Section 1

Why Not Yet?

God created SEX. People are "hush hush" about that word! There would be NO people on earth if it was not for sex. What GOD gives, the enemy, satan would like to <u>DESTROY</u>!! Your body is <u>sacred</u>, Yes, SACRED! It is NOT up for "grabs" Some have destroyed their lives because of "<u>experimenting</u>." Sex is to be <u>SAVED</u> for <u>marriage</u>. If you <u>owned</u> a beautiful exquisite diamond ring, would you give it to any old rubby dub? NO! NO!

Chapter 1

Timing Is Everything

"Go!"

Sprinters in the starting blocks before a race are *ready*. They're *set*, and every nerve in their body is screaming, "Go!" But their minds are trained to override the urge. They're fully aware that pushing off before the starter's last command could cost them the race.

If you've watched Olympic track and field or other competitive races, you've no doubt seen some false starts. Since the introduction of the brutal "one-and-done" false start rule, I always find the beginning of a race nerve-racking. The rules changed in 2010. No second chance in the same race. One false start and the athlete is disqualified! *What if their timing is off?* The question runs through my mind over and over. Then a desperate, all-consuming plea follows: *Please don't false start! Please don't! Pleeeease!*

The way I feel about you is no different. You see, I know the urges to "run" into sexual activities can be very intense at your age. I recognize that as an adolescent, when it comes to your sexuality, you're either about to enter or are already in an intense competitive race: a showdown between the morals you may have been taught about sex and marriage on the one hand, and on the other, your own desires and what's popular in the culture.

Like a champion sprinter in the starting blocks, you're **"Ready"** because God created you male or female with sexual desires. You get **“Set”** when these desires awaken at puberty or earlier. But unlike the sprinter, what’s next for you isn’t “Go!” What follows is **“Not Yet!”** Timing is everything. Figuring out how to keep your feet grounded in those blocks will makes a world of difference. Let’s figure it out together!

Olympic sprinters are often icons of self-control and patience. And even for the best of them, avoiding a false start is easier said than done. To get an appreciation of how intentional and focused you’ll need to be in your pursuit of sexual wholeness, I’m inviting you for the next few moments to dive into the world of a sprinter and imagine yourself at the peak of your career.

Let’s Imagine

It’s finally here! The moment you dreamed of all your life. You’ve worked tirelessly, investing everything into this opportunity. You’re about to run your first race in an Olympics finals. You’re going for gold. You’re in tip top shape, and your performance in the preliminaries has you tagged as the winner. Grapevine even has it that there’s money on you. A lot is riding on these next few minutes, but you’ve got this!

The echo of the first command releases an instant adrenalin rush:

“ON YOUR MARKS ...”

You’ve practised the starting commands hundreds of times, perhaps even thousands. But this isn’t a rehearsal. It’s real! You appreciate the pause before the next command. These few seconds are like gold. Time to collect your nerves and bring your whole being into alignment. Shuffle. The ritualistic shaking of your hands and feet. Self-talk: *Not Yet! Focus! Relax!*

“SET ...”

More golden seconds follow, giving you a chance to prepare for your best start. You’re smack in the middle of the greatest moment of the competition—not the race against the other sprinters on your left and right. The greatest competition is within, against yourself, your own thoughts. The battle between anxiety and patience is fierce. You side with patience. Patience must win. Patience knows that it must wait for the final command. That's the rule. No way around it. More self-talk: *Disqualification is NOT an option!*

You're torn between appreciation of these precious seconds before the final command and frustration that the wait is too long. Oh yes, the starter knows you're not quite set. So just a few more seconds of shuffling. A few more seconds to really get set.

In your mind's eye you see your first medal . . . GOLD! It hangs elegantly around your neck, glittering in the sun's brilliant rays. You assure yourself: *I've got this!*

Then ...

In a moment of unrestrained passion and broken concentration, you push off.

"Grrrrrr!!!! Oh no! How could ... I ... Howwww ...?"

You wish it was a bad dream and you'd wake up from it. But it's not. You just had a false start. You lost the race before it even began. You know you're disqualified with no second chance for this race. The mistake of not waiting just a few more seconds cost you the opportunity of a lifetime.

Now a Real Scenario

The year is 2011. The place is South Korea. The occasion is the International Association of Athletics Federation (IAAF) World Championships. The athletic event is the 100-metre final. Usain Bolt is the main attraction, defending his title as the fastest man in the world with a 9.58 world record.

The build-up to the race is electrifying. Cameras. Thousands of onsite spectators. Loud cheers and flags everywhere. Millions are watching by television and online. The competing athletes position themselves in their assigned lane as every word from the commentator heightens the suspense.

The race of all races is about to begin. A piercing silence follows the echo of the first and second commands: "ON YOUR MARKS ..." "SET ..."

Then ...

Horror of all horrors. Usain Bolt leapt from his starting blocks. The commentator's first words captured the horrific moment: "Oh no! Massive, massive disappointment ... and he knows it too!"

Yes, Usain Bolt knew it—he was out! One false start with no second chance to defend his title in this race. He whisked off his vest immediately, threw it to the ground, and started pacing, dazed by what had just happened. His hands moved through seemingly programmed motions: covering his mouth, then his face, then cradling the back of his head. His eyes flashed away into the distance, then with head thrown back, he turned his gaze upward before walking off the field.

Disqualified! Usain Bolt, the Lightning Bolt, forced to sit out the race. How did that happen? Technically, he had pushed off within the 0.10 seconds disqualification window (which for our purposes is the *"Not Yet!"* zone).

Usain had supported the introduction of the new "one-and-done" false start rule. So although disappointed, he graciously accepted the disqualification without criticizing the authorities.

Knowing the rules and fully supporting them didn't make it any easier for Usain to follow them in that moment. Hmmm. That's an important principle right there, and you'll want to take special note of it.

Fun Fact

"This 0.10 seconds figure is based on a research which says that reaction time faster than one-tenth of a second is impossible for humans. As such, the sprinter is thus deemed to have anticipated the gun."[1]

Aha! Moments

It was heartbreaking to watch Usain Bolt's false start. But the heartbreak led to an Aha! moment. It was as if the lights were turned on. Similar to the rules and consequences in the world of sports, it made sense that sex, which was created by God for a sacred purpose, has a "wait for marriage" rule. In Section 2 you'll find out more about God's sacred purpose for sex.

I also had another insightful moment during a conversation with a friend who was a former sprinter. She shared with me that undetected false starts happen all the time. Some athletes are so conditioned and skilled in timing techniques that by a mental count they know the split second to push off without being detected. How clever!

Well, athletes may get away with undetected false starts, but it's often not that simple when it comes to sexual false starts. Although undetected by others, their consequences still play out in one way or another. Thinking about undetected sexual false starts also made me think of something you may have heard before: Don't play with fire!

Waiting Makes All the Difference

Waiting makes all the difference for a sprinter in the starting blocks. Waiting makes all the difference for you too as you battle the fierce competition of sexual pressures. As one young adult said about her teenage sexual false starts, "I knew the rules, but waiting was my Achilles heel."

You may be wondering whether it's possible to really wait for marriage before having sex. The short answer is yes. Let me explain, reaching back to what you just read about the IAAF. They had introduced the "one-and-done" false start rule knowing that with the updated technology built into starting blocks, it's possible for sprinters to avoid false starts.

Similarly, the Creator of sex made the "sex for marriage" rule because He knows it's possible. Jesus said it this way: "Anything is possible if a person believes."[2] As you see, it has a lot to do with what you believe, especially about yourself, God, and about His plan for your sexuality. Here's something important for you to keep believing. Your Heavenly Father loves you so much that He makes His power (grace) available to you to work in you and do what you cannot do in your own strength.

Your cooperation is still necessary in order to benefit from God's grace while waiting. Your thought life and what you choose to set your mind on is vital during this time. You see, your actions will always follow your most dominant thought, meaning you will eventually false start if you're accustomed to entertaining sexual thoughts and fantasies. You'll need to cultivate the discipline of self-control in your thought life by choosing to set your mind on things that will strengthen your resistance against temptations. I know it's easier said than done, but the key is in this one word: Reboot!

Be prepared and willing to reboot your mind by replacing tempting thoughts and images with words and affirmations that empower you to follow God's "sex for marriage" design. The "Words to Live By" reflections at the end of each chapter will help you do just that. Good news! You're able to access all "Words to Live By" in one place under the "Reboot Your Mind Collection" in the Bonus Section at the end of the book.

Among other things, waiting provides an opportunity for you to experience greater dependency on the Lord. King David, who is described in the Bible as the greatest of all kings, knew this well. He had learned to wait and depend on God early in life as a young shepherd boy. This is what this great king had to say about his waiting experience: "Here's what I've learned through it all: Don't give up; don't be impatient; be entwined as one with the Lord. Be brave and courageous, and never lose hope. Yes, keep on waiting—for he will never disappoint you!" [3]

In a practical sense, waiting will also provide you with an opportunity for greater preparation. We'll check that out in the next chapter. First a pause for reflections. Oh, and don't forget that you can use the lines provided to express your thoughts in your own words.

Chapter 1 Reflections

Did you know?	Training your mind is the key to overriding sexual urges in the *Not Yet!* zone.
Words to Live By	I can do everything through Christ, who gives me strength! (Philippians 4:13, NLT) "Relationships are most fulfilled when we follow the advice 'not to awaken love until the time is right.'" (Pam Stenzel)
From Your Heart	**Your Prayer:** Heavenly Father, please help me to truly believe in my heart that waiting in the *Not Yet!* zone is possible. Help me to depend on your strength as I wait. I ask this in the Name of Jesus. Amen.

Chapter 2

Waiting Is for Preparation

Waiting is difficult. I agree. However, my overall perspective about waiting changed significantly when I learned that waiting isn't a passive waste of time. There's more to waiting than just waiting. As it is for a sprinter in the starting blocks, waiting will create a "space" for your preparation.

You may recall me saying earlier that the image of the sprint athlete in the starting blocks is an excellent metaphor for the moment-by-moment choices you'll make about sex as a teenager. This image is a perfect picture of you waiting for marriage before getting into sexual activities. You see, sex before marriage is like showing up to engage in a race when you haven't trained or prepared for it. Actually, you're not even a "registered" competitor. In other words, you're not yet ready. Waiting in the *Not Yet!* zone is a gift in disguise, although you may not realize it. Most times, waiting doesn't feel like something good, but it aligns you with God's timing and gets you ready. Waiting is for preparation, and preparation is a prerequisite for victory.

Jackie Joyner-Kersee is a retired champion track and field athlete with three gold, one silver, and two bronze Olympic medals.[4] She has a great piece of advice for you about preparation: "It's better to look ahead and prepare than to look back and regret." [5]

Athletes in Waiting

Watching Olympic races, it's impossible to miss how focused the athletes are in those few seconds before the race officially starts. But what we don't get to see is what's involved in the years of waiting before getting to the Olympics. I've heard that Olympic athletes prepare an average of four to eight years for only a few minutes of competition. Math isn't my forte, so I don't know what that ratio would be. I just know it's so out of proportion! And it gets even more absurd. Some athletes start dreaming from childhood about being an Olympian. For these athletes, it's not only a few years. It's their entire life that's spent preparing for one moment in time.

Finding out how Olympians and other champion athletes prepare during their waiting years will certainly provide much needed insights for this *Not Yet!* zone of your teenage journey. Their preparation obviously involves intense technical skills training. But that's not all. Preparation also requires the painstaking development of a certain kind of lifestyle and mindset.

Here's a picture of dedicated athletes. We're going to examine six areas that are highly relevant to you, especially when it comes to how you see yourself and the kind of choices you make.

Vision	Olympic and other champion athletes carry a vision or mental picture of their future imprinted on their hearts and minds. For example, many Olympians see themselves competing in the Olympics long before they get there. The mental picture they have of their future ignites laser-focused passion. In the language of the Bible, it's "the joy set before them."[6] Vision empowers them with endurance and perseverance to resist distractions and overcome challenges.

Faith Champion athletes see through eyes of faith. They're people of faith, although they may not be religious in the traditional sense of the word. It's not unusual, however, to find athletes who believe and rely on the power of God to be at their best. Once while watching some swimmers train at the York University pool, I saw these words tattooed across a young man's back: "Zechariah 4:6 By the Spirit of the Lord." Clearly, he was making it known, even reminding himself of the spiritual source that fuels his inner strength and performance.

Winning Winning is the single word that best describes the mindset of champion athletes. Having a winning attitude or mindset means they don't give in to challenges. Instead of allowing challenges to overcome them, they do their best to turn challenges into opportunities for growth. Because winning is such a priority, they willingly follow the established rules for their sport to avoid penalties and disqualification. In fact, they see the rules as beneficial—a way of leveling the playing field.

Discipline Champion athletes have a disciplined lifestyle. They even pay attention to what they put in their bodies. They follow strict, regimented training routines and invest most of their time into skills development and practising. Mental fitness, patience, and right thinking are also a high priority, so they exercise self-control to master not only their bodies but their thoughts as well. We could say that successful athletes are positive thinkers. They know that without mental and physical discipline they will be easily overcome by distractions.

Commitment They live fully committed to the picture they have in their mind of themselves as a champion athlete. This passionate commitment enables them to willingly impose self-contraints and endure challenges of all kinds. They undergo rigorous training to be successful. They're also committed to developing strong relationships with coaches and others to whom they're accountable for personal and professional development.

Sacrifice The lifestyle of champion athletes is a great example of sacrificial love—love for the sport, and a passion for personal success. Their desire to enhance the sport and team they represent fuels their lifestyle. They also put high value on the privilege of representing their country. They choose delayed gratification and personal restraint to avoid anything that could potentially sabotage their future as a champion. They willingly sacrifice short-term pleasures for long-term gain.

Preparation Secrets from the Life of An Athlete

A secret is simply something hidden from others. You may have seen many Olympic races and not give much thought to what's behind the stellar performance of the athletes. Now the secret's out! Just by looking briefly at the six key areas above, you have more insight into what's involved. But how do these areas apply to you?

Let's do a quick personal check-up using a scale of 1–5 (low to high). How prepared would you say you are for your teenage journey in these six areas?

How clear is your mental picture of your future?

1 2 3 4 5

How strong is your faith in your potential to do great things?

1 2 3 4 5

How willing are you to follow God's ways (go by the rules) in order to win in life?

1 2 3 4 5

How disciplined are you?

1 2 3 4 5

How committed are you to a lifestyle of sexual wholeness?

1 2 3 4 5

How willing are you to give up short-term pleasures for long-term gain?

1 2 3 4 5

Your Preparation Waiting Plan

How was your personal checkup? The idea of the exercise isn't for you to be discouraged but to identify areas you need to focus on sooner rather than later. I encourage you to start developing a Preparation Waiting Plan. Use your notebook or device for this purpose. Ask yourself questions like:

- What will I do to move higher on the scale for each of the above areas?
- What academic, career, spiritual, and other goals do I want to accomplish in life?
- How can I make the best use of my waiting time before marriage?
- Who will I ask questions or invite to support me?
- What activities will I avoid during this time?
- Which Bible verses will I meditate on?[7]
- How do I expect my waiting time to benefit me?

At first it may feel awkward when you start writing down your thoughts, but it does get easier the more you do it, so keep going. This plan is primarily for you. However, remember that it will be helpful at some point to share it with a parent, youth leader, or mentor who will provide much needed support. In Section 3 you'll find concrete suggestions to help you build on these thoughts.

A Biblical Perspective

Let me end this chapter with a perspective from scripture. Did you know that even in the Bible athletes are icons of a disciplined lifestyle? In the following verses, the Apostle Paul compares his own spiritual journey and that of others to a competitive race:

Isn't it obvious that all runners on the racetrack keep on running to win, but only one receives the victor's prize? Yet each one of you must run the race to be victorious. A true athlete will be disciplined in every respect, practicing constant self-control in order to win a laurel wreath that quickly withers. But we run our race to win a victor's crown that will last forever. For that reason, I don't run just for exercise or box like one throwing aimless punches, but ***I train like a champion athlete. I subdue my body and get it under my control,*** *so that after* *preaching the good news to others I myself won't be disqualified.* (1 Corinthians 9:24–27, TPT, emphasis mine)

God sees you as a champion in your own right. Seeing the sexual aspects of your teenage journey in the context of an athlete's lifestyle and mindset does make good sense. Gold medals are a great reward for the investment that Olympians and others make in their athletic career. We could say then that a gold medal is a reward for diligent preparation. Also, in the case of a champion sprinter, the gold medal certainly rewards the athlete's discipline of waiting for the starter's command to avoid a false start and disqualification.

Like these champion athletes, you're going for gold! Sexual wholeness is the "gold medal" you're reaching for. In the next chapter, you'll read about another perspective on waiting, which will help you further understand that it pays to wait.

Chapter 2 Reflections

Did you know?	Using your waiting time in the *Not Yet!* zone for preparation is like a financial investment that yields extremely high returns.
Words to Live By	And let us run with perseverance the race marked out for us, fixing our eyes on Jesus, the pioneer and perfecter of faith. For the joy set before him he endured the cross. (Hebrews 12:1–2) An athlete who refuses to play by the rules will never get anywhere. (2 Timothy 2:5, The Message)
From Your Heart	**Your Prayer:** Heavenly Father, I realize that you know everything about me and the specific ways that I need to prepare myself to experience sexual wholeness. In the Name of Jesus, I'm asking for your help in areas where I'm weak. Amen.

Chapter 3

It's Worth the Wait

"Here is a marshmallow. You can eat it now or you can wait until I get back and have two marshmallows."

You may recognize these words from the famous Marshmallow Test, which leaves four to eight-year-olds in a room for a few minutes with a marshmallow, a choice, and a promise. Will they wait or will they give in? The experiment aims to teach children the discipline of self-control— that making a sacrifice now will pay off later.

The experiences of the children from the marshmallow experiment and the sprinter in the starting blocks convey the same message to you as a teenager: Self-control pays, but instant gratification will cost you. Although you may not see it that way now, the truth is that you'll end up better off all round if you wait for marriage and experience sex God's way.

Children in Waiting

I watched a few YouTube videos of the marshmallow experiment and was fascinated by how the boys and girls responded to the temptation of being left alone with the marshmallow. Some verbalized what they were thinking, but most spoke with their eyes and facial expressions. Magnetic gazes that if possible, would have pulled the marshmallow off the plate, puzzled brows from brains hard at work, and eager eyes twinkling with intrigue exposed their thoughts:

Well, I'm hungry and I can't wait.

I've never had a marshmallow before. I wonder how it tastes.

It looks so squishy ... It must be good!

The brave ones picked up the marshmallow, smelled it, licked it, poked it, and rolled it in their hands. Others hummed and tapped their hands as they stared patiently. One boy found a creative solution. He turned the marshmallow into an imaginary car and enjoyed the pleasure of driving it back and forth on the table. Their expressions were priceless: boredom, curiosity, and frustration. A few watched the door, desperate for the ordeal to end. Of course, some ate the marshmallow. One of the boys took such a tiny piece of the marshmallow it was barely noticeable. It made me think of a sprinter's undetected false start.

The waiting experiences of these children are good illustrations of what sexual temptation may look like in the *Not Yet!* zone. How far can I go? How far is too far? I often hear these questions from young people. These children in the experiment basically struggled with the same questions.

The FloodSanDiego Video

This episode with a boy and girl in the FloodSanDiego YouTube video is my favourite. [8]

The facilitator of the experiment left them together in the room with a clear instruction: "So I have one marshmallow for each of you. And here's the deal. You can either eat it now or wait until I get back and you can have two." She repeated herself just to be sure they got it.

The boy made his position clear as soon as the door closed ... well, sort of: "We're going to wait, right?"

The girl agreed. "We're gonna wait."

His next question exposed his inner struggle: "I wonder what we're going to do?" He lifted himself up from his chair, glanced at the marshmallow in the girl's plate, and asked yet another question: "Are you going to eat it?"

Before his last word was out, the girl picked up her marshmallow and bit into it. "I just want to take one bite," she explained as she chewed on the tasty tidbit.

He then tried to convince her. "But if you wait until she gets back, she'll give you two."

Too late. She had already taken another bite.

He pointed to the mangled remains of the marshmallow on her plate and reminded her of the consequence: "She still won't give you two because you ate it ... some of it." Then he picked up his marshmallow and proudly asserted, "And I didn't eat a single bite."

At this point, the girl's face was almost buried in her plate. Wanting to help her out, the boy came up with a solution: "So don't show her, okay!" But as far as he was concerned, his mind was now fully made up, and he made it known. "I'm waiting," he said.

The girl liked his confidence, so she copied him. "I'm waiting too!"

The boy corrected her. "Well ... no ... you're eating ... not waiting for her to get back."

"I can wait," she replied softly.

"Well, you still ate some of it, so she's still not going to give you two." The girl started to get out of her chair while whispering something, to which the boy responded, "No, stay in your chair."

She continued toward the door, and as she opened it, the facilitator walked in. Surprised to meet the girl at the door, she asked, "Oh, what happened?" The girl just sheepishly looked at her as she nervously twirled the bottom of her blouse.

Instantly the boy tattled: "She ate hers!"

Mixed Emotions

When the episode ended, I couldn't stop the wave of sadness I felt for the little girl and her loss. I felt her aloneness, and I imagined her staring grudgingly at the boy receiving and enjoying his second marshmallow. I imagined her wishing that she had waited. While part of me celebrated the boy's victory, I was disappointed that in the end, he didn't support the girl. I thought that he could have waited for her to own up to what happened, then supported her by saying something like, "She really tried, but it was so difficult."

In the boy's response I saw something that's important for you to remember as a teenager—friends may not always be supportive when you're facing the consequences of your choices. Teens often face the consequences of a sexual false start alone and disappointed, just like a sprinter who walks away from the track after having a false start. The fan club and cheering party are nowhere to be found. Young ladies, if you'll allow me to be honest with you here, sometimes even the one(s) with whom you had the sexual encounter may do a disappearing act. Whether you're male or female, you may find yourself struggling on your own with feelings of guilt, shame, anger, and disappointment, especially after you've done something you had promised yourself not to do.

Well, who did you identify with in the marshmallow experiment? The boy or the girl? Why? If you identified more with the girl, let me remind you that this little girl would have opportunities to prepare for other "marshmallow tests." She'd have a chance to start building her self-control muscles. The same goes for you. Yielding to temptation once doesn't mean you always will. You can use the experience as fuel for your self-control training and preparation. What if you identified with the boy? Be alert because overcoming temptation once doesn't mean you always will. And don't forget to be there for your friends when they're facing the consequences of their choices.

How Did They Do It?

I understand that only about one-third of children who participate in Marshmallow Tests don't eat the marshmallow. Why are some able to wait and not others? Any number of factors may have been at work. I suspect that those who waited had some previous "training." When faced with the marshmallow, the skill of self discipline wasn't new for them. It may have begun at home, school, or elsewhere. It may even have been in little things that they learned the valuable lesson of associating choices with consequences. In other words, they had already started to learn that short-term sacrifices produce long-term gain.

Some of the children who waited also explained that they used their imagination to help them wait. They imagined the marshmallow to be something unpleasant, or they imagined themselves enjoying two marshmallows instead of one. Saving sex for marriage is like enjoying two marshmallows! While in the *Not Yet!* zone of your teenage journey, you also have a choice in how you use your gift of imagination. Allowing the Holy Spirit to inspire how you use this gift from God will help you make wise sexual choices.

What's The Big Deal About Self-Control?

Self-control has to do with will-power. It's one of the most difficult disciplines to develop but perhaps the most important. Recently I was with a group of ladies in a situation that called for extreme patience. I heard this statement for the first time: "Hurry up and wait." What a paradox! It captures in a nutshell what the sexual part of your teenage journey is all about.

Developing self-control at an early age will impact just about every area of your life as a teenager, from academic performance to choices about sex. And get this—the benefit goes far beyond your teen years. Walter Mischel, the inventor of the Marshmallow Test, says it like this: "If you do exhibit self-control at an early age, you have a much better chance of taking the future into account, and likely to have better outcomes."[9]

Sesame Street was at one time the most popular children's program on television. If you ever watched the program, I'm sure you'll remember

Cookie Monster and his out-of-control behaviour. His famous chant was about wanting the cookie and wanting it NOW! Well, guess what? Even Cookie Monster came around to learning self-control. He's been transformed! Here's his new message that's had almost 15 million views on YouTube: *"Me want it but me wait. Me wait. Me can self-regulate. #controlmeself."*[10] I believe those are good mottos for sexual choices. Don't you?

What If ...?

So what if you didn't wait for the second marshmallow? What if you've already had a false start in your sexual journey? What if you have a false start down the road? Questions like these helped to inspire *Ready. Set. Not Yet!* I've heard them many times from young people like yourself. My answer: Reset is possible!

Driving to new places, especially on the highway, I sometimes miss my exit and end up completely off track. But regardless of how far I get off course, I can depend on the Google GPS to reroute me and keep me on track. The chapters in Section 3 are your *Ready. Set. Not Yet!* "Spiritual GPS." They're loaded with helpful practical strategies to help you reset and reroute after a false start. Better yet, they include strategies for waiting successfully in the *Not Yet!* zone.

What's Next?

Before getting into the strategies, we're going to first explore the spiritual mysteries about sex. Because you're growing up at the height of the information age, your generation is perhaps the most sexually aware of any generation. With the internet, search engines, and social media, you have so much at your fingertips that hardly anything is hidden about the physical aspects of sex. But so very little is known about this important truth: There's more to sex than just the physical act.

You see, sex is a mystery, and much of the mystery is spiritual. The secret to the mystery can only be found in the thoughts and heart of its inventor—God. Although you may have access to tons of information about sex, there's something extremely important for you to realize. Not just any information or opinion is going to prepare you to victoriously overcome the many sexual struggles you'll be facing. There's plenty to discover about the non-physical (spiritual) side of sex. To reach the goal of sexual wholeness, it's going to be essential for you to understand the spiritual mysteries about sex. I'm convinced that having this understanding will provide you with a more compelling reason to save sex for marriage.

So far, you've had the opportunity to put yourself in the place of athletes and waiting children. Get ready to explore in the next section the *Big Ideas* God had in mind when He invented sex. But first you'll be reading a story from my childhood and early teen years. Growing up, I knew nothing about the spiritual mysteries that you'll be discovering here in *Ready. Set. Not Yet!* Neither did most adults, for that matter. They knew about the physical aspects only but turned even that part into a mystery for the younger generation. You'll read more on that later.

I know you'll want to get to the story. Just before that, though, please take the time to complete the reflection and take-away exercises.

Chapter 3 Reflections

Did you know? Self-control is like a muscle, and it's never too late to start building that muscle.

Words to Live By A person without self-control is like a city with broken-down walls. (Proverbs 25:28, NLT)

"Self-control is not the ability to say no to a thousand other voices. It is the ability to say yes to the one thing so completely that there's nothing left to give to the other options." (Bill Johnson)

From Your Heart **Your Prayer:** Heavenly Father, I ask for your strength to say "yes" to your will and your way when I'm tempted to act on the sexual urges in my body. Please help me to remember that the sacrifices I make now will later produce great reward. Thank you for helping me!

____

____

____

____

____

____

____

____

____

Section 1 Take-Aways

The Main Thing

Read these key points from the section and circle a number from 1–5 to indicate how much you have embraced each truth. *("1" is "I totally disagree" and "5" is "I agree completely.")*

Highlight the key points with a score of 3 or less and make them the focus of your prayer practice below.

My waiting in the *Not Yet!* zone isn't a passive waste of time. It's for my preparation.

1 2 3 4 5

Self-control pays, but instant gratification will cost me.

1 2 3 4 5

Yielding to temptation once doesn't mean I always will. Nor does overcoming temptation once mean I always will. I must stay alert.

1 2 3 4 5

There's more to sex than just the physical act.

1 2 3 4 5

I may have access to tons of information about sex, but not just any information or opinion will prepare me to victoriously overcome the sexual struggles I experience.

1 2 3 4 5

The Main Thing (cont'd)

Reaching the goal of sexual wholeness requires that I understand the spiritual mysteries about sex.

1 2 3 4 5

Sexual wholeness is the "gold medal" I'm reaching for.

1 2 3 4 5

Similar to the rules and consequences in the world of sports, it makes sense that God has a "wait for marriage" rule for something as sacred as sex.

1 2 3 4 5

My Heavenly Father loves me so much that He gives me His power (grace) to accomplish in me what I can't do in my own strength.

1 2 3 4 5

Prayer Practice

Speak to your Heavenly Father and ask Him to help you with the key points above that you need to internalize more fully. You may wish to write your prayer, and remember to include anyone who may be having similar challenges.

Your Call to Action *Identify at least one action you're committed to taking based on something you discovered in this section. Remember to use your "memory tools."*

____

____

____

____

____

____

____

A Blessing Beloved teen, I bless you with the gift of self-control to wait on your Heavenly Father's perfect timing instead of trying to satisfy your immediate desires. May you not allow the world around you to influence you. Instead, may you develop a trained mind to align your body with God's intent and purposes. I bless you with the assurance that you have what it takes to wait on God's perfect timing for marriage, knowing that His reward will be well worth the wait. You're blessed in the Name of the Lord. *(Bite-Size Blessing Power Edition: Perfect Timing)*[11]

Section 2

There's More to Sex

Kendal: Any gift God gives us, satan desecrates, uses it against us and turns God's TRUTH into a lie. Satan is the King of liars!

Chapter 4

Airplanes and Kisses

I discovered sex "accidentally." Let me tell you how it happened. I suspect that after reading my story, you'll be thinking, *That's crazy ... messed up ... ridiculous*. And that's okay, as I see it that way myself.

The setting is my back yard in Jamaica with a bunch of seven, eight, and nine-year-old girls playing and waiting for my new baby brother or sister to arrive. We were outside for hours, and every so often an adult peeked through the back door to make sure we were okay. Normally the door would've been opened for us to go in and out of the house as we wished, but all the doors were locked on this day. My mother and a few other women were huddled inside, one of them in a white dress like a nurse. I was the first to get to the door each time it opened. I could hardly wait to find out whether the "airplane" had brought me a baby brother or sister.

Finally, my grandma broke the news. It wasn't good. The airplane came with a baby brother but dropped him and he died. Uhhhh! My grandma closed the door just as quickly as she had opened it. I could tell that she was hurrying back to something important.

I leaned against the locked door with tears tumbling from my broken heart and streaming down my cheeks. One of the girls from next door walked over and stood beside me for a moment. She started talking, and I quickly realized that she was there to set me straight, not to comfort me. "Babies don't come from airplanes. Babies come from your mother's belly." Of course, she said it in our local language: "*Baby nuh cum fram noh airplane. Baby cum fram yuh madda belly.*"

She sounded so convincing that I believed every word. But I was so shocked I didn't even think of asking her how they got there. I couldn't bear the thought, however, that my grandmother had lied, so I settled for another option—Grandma had "fooled me." She said something untrue but with good intentions.

I had stumbled on what turned out to be my introductory lesson to sex and babies. Unclear, mysterious, and confusing. Sex Education 101 with an accidental twist!

Years later, in my early teens and after my monthly periods had started, I got an upgraded lesson from my mother. Hers wasn't much better. This time, she "fooled me" about pregnancy. She gave me a stern warning. "Do not kiss boys, for you will get pregnant and have a baby!" I wondered whether this was a piece of the puzzle that my friend had left out. Kissing. Pregnancy. Babies. Was that it? I wasn't sure, but the thought of having a baby scared the wits out of me, so I chose to believe what my mother said.

I was horrified the first time I dared kissed a boy (and it wasn't even a real kiss!) Seeing the horror that came over me, he quickly set me straight when I told him about my mother's warning.

"You won't get pregnant," he jeered. "You have to have sex first."

Sex? Aha! So that's it! The dots finally connected after he explained what having sex meant.

I had a little diary at the time that I really treasured. I only wished it had a lock. I thought this first kiss deserved an entry, so I gladly wrote: "He kissed me and walked me home." A few months later, I spent some time with an elderly cousin who lived in another part of the island and forgot my diary at her home. She read it and found out about the kiss, so she sent a telegram to my mother saying it was urgent. She was to come quickly and take me along. (We didn't yet have the convenience of telephones, and a telegram was the fastest way to send messages over long distances.) The strap was my punishment for being so daring, but it was still without clear explanation. They didn't tell me the truth—that I couldn't get pregnant by kissing a boy.

Looking back at that experience as a teenager, I'm not surprised by the passion I now have for sharing the spiritual mysteries about sex with your generation. You deserve to know sooner rather than later. Although you have access to more information about sex than I had at your age, without an understanding of the spiritual mysteries, you're no better prepared than I was to overcome the sexual challenges of your teen years.

Why They (We) Did It

Why did my grandma, mother, and cousin hide the truth about sex and babies? Why did they make the physical act of sex so mysterious? They did it for the same reason that many adults of this generation still do. I must confess that I also foolishly did the same thing when I had my children. We had no idea about the spiritual mystery of sex but felt that what we knew about the physical act was worth hiding. We just couldn't get past our embarrassment, discomfort, and, most of all, our fears.

I've thought a lot about this. I think I've figured out some of the reasons why we hid the truth:

- When my mother told me that kissing would make me pregnant, she wasn't afraid of the act of kissing. She was afraid of what it could lead to.
- We were afraid that our children would experiment with sex. We learned that neither silence, lies, scare tactics, nor rules made much of a difference. They did anyway.

- We couldn't resolve some of our own conflicting views about sex and our bodies. Labels like "dirty" and "not good" were often attached to sex and our bodies. Yet we knew there was also pleasure, and that sex was God's way of bringing children into the world.
- We just didn't know how to talk about these things—when to begin, where to begin, and how much to tell. In the end, we did what we thought was best for everyone.

I'm not trying to defend the generations I represent by sharing these thoughts with you. I sincerely apologize for our silence, misrepresentations, and unreasonable expectations, which did more harm than good.

You're a History Maker

I did my undergraduate degree in history, not realizing that one day I'd become a history maker who inspires future history makers. We can't change the past, but we can all learn from it and rewrite the script going forward. *Ready. Set. Not Yet!* is a gift from the generations I represent. You've received it to prepare you for the responsibility of living and passing on a healthy sexual inheritance to your future children. I wrote this book not because I'm an expert, or because I got it all right. It's the opposite. My passion is that you won't repeat the mistakes that I and others made as teenagers and young adults. "I missed it, but you don't have to" is one of my mottos, and you'll find it popping up throughout the book.

You truly are a budding history maker, and I bless you with all the wisdom, courage, and confidence you'll need to maximize your potential and fulfill the great purpose for which you were born.

Chapter 4 Reflections

Did you know?	Although it's more subtle, popular cultural views and opinions about sex may be "fooling you" just as the adults in my generation fooled me.
Words to Live By	Humanly speaking, no one can understand the mysteries of God without the Holy Spirit. (1 Corinthians 2:16, TPT footnote) Trust in the Lord completely, and do not rely on your own opinions. (Proverbs 3:5a, TPT)
From Your Heart	**Your Prayer:** Heavenly Father, I call out to you. Make my mind ready to receive wisdom and revelation so I'll truly know you and understand your ways. Open the eyes of my heart, and let the light of your truth flood in. Thank you for providing everything I need to become the history maker you've chosen me to be. I pray this in the Name of Jesus. Amen.

____

____

____

____

____

Chapter 5

God's Big Ideas

"I want to know God's thoughts—the rest are details." That's a quote from the genius Albert Einstein, whose discoveries and theories changed the scientific world. I like the quote because its wisdom applies to every area of life.

As a scientist, Einstein wanted to know the secrets that the Creator had built into the universe. Once he knew the Creator's intentions, he could figure out the details of how the universe was supposed to work, and how to experience its best. Likewise, because sex is God's invention, knowing His intentions or ideas about sex will help you to experience your sexuality God's way—the best way!

Discovering More from The Creator

There's more to sex than the messages you pick up from social media, movies, music, friends, and other sources. The only place to discover the "more" is from the mind of God the Creator. Some of the information in this section may be new to you, but that's okay because that's what discovery is about—finding out what you didn't know before.

The Bible is the best place to start discovering what was in the mind of God about humanity, including His intentions or ideas about sex and sexuality. The first thing to note is that the Bible is essentially a book about a divine romance—God's love for humanity. Although you may not have heard this truth before, God loves you passionately, and that means you are centre stage in His great love story. But to understand this love story, you'll need to be aware that the Bible uses visible images to explain what is invisible. It also uses many metaphors to illustrate and simplify deep and complex principles. The application icons on a smart phone work like that too. A big part of understanding the Bible is asking God to help you figure out the deeper meanings of its many images and metaphors.

What's The Big Idea?

You may have been wondering what's the big deal about not having sex before marriage. Well, it really is a big deal because it's God's *Big Idea*. This chapter presents ten of God's *Big Ideas* from the Bible that will help to clarify the spiritual mystery about sex and human sexuality.

They'll answer questions such as: Why does God care so much about sex and marriage? Why did God create me male or female? Why do my sexual desires seem to have a life of their own?

#1BigIdea	Your existence begins in God because of His love.
#2BigIdea	God is Spirit, He is eternal (exists outside of time), and He expresses Himself as Father, Son, and Holy Spirit. The three exist as one in an intimate union of endless love that's pure, holy, undefiled, beautiful, and good.
#3BigIdea	God's ultimate purpose for creating human beings is for us to also exist with Him in this same intimate union of endless love.
#4BigIdea	God made your body for the grand purpose of being the majestic, holy habitation of His Spirit now and for eternity (forever).
#5BigIdea	God created you a male or female sexual being with longings for intimacy wired into your body. He designed your body with these longings to mirror the deeper spiritual need you have for union with God, to know Him intimately and to be known by Him.

#6BigIdea The ingrained passion of the human heart for endless union with God, and our capacity for intimate relationship with God and others, set us apart from animals.

#7BigIdea The sexual urges in your body aren't just physical longings for sex. They point to the desire all humans have from God to be truly known, loved, and accepted in relationship just for who we are.

#8BigIdea The marriage of a man and woman is an earthly icon pointing to the heavenly marriage and intimacy between God and humanity that will last for all eternity.

#9BigIdea God designed sex and marriage to go together, with marriage as a covenant (permanent promise) between a man and woman. God's intent is for the marriage covenant to provide a safe, healthy, lasting environment for true intimacy and for raising godly children.

#10BigIdea You're created for an eternal spiritual destination beyond your present physical existence that's limited in time.

Bible Credits *Genesis 1–2; John 4:24; Deuteronomy 6:4; 1 John 4:7; 1 Corinthians 3:16, 1 Corinthians 6:19–20; Matthew 19:8; Malachi 2:15; Ephesians 5:31; Revelation 19:6–9.*

I realize there was a lot to absorb in the *Big Ideas* you just read. I suggest reading them over and looking up the Bible references.

True Intimacy

Prior to reading those *Big Ideas,* intimacy may not have been something you associated with God. It may even feel a bit strange to do that now. I understand. In the natural sense, intimacy has come to represent mostly nakedness and physical sexual acts. But as you've now discovered, there's more to intimacy. Intimacy originated in God as an expression of the union of pure endless love shared by God the Father, Son, and Holy Spirit. It's also an expression of the same union that God created us to share with Him.

You also now understand that the sexual urges you experience in your body are part of God's design. You need not be afraid of them. God didn't put them there to tempt or frustrate you. Neither are they meant to be green light signals for sexual activities. They serve the greater purpose of pointing you to the intimate bond of endless love with God for which He created you.

Spirit, Soul, and Body

I'll be bold in saying that I'm sure you now know more about the significance of your body than you did at the start of the chapter. Am I right or not? The understanding you've gained will certainly guide you in your pursuit of sexual wholeness. Still, I want you to know that as valuable as your body is, it represents only part of who you are. In other words, you're not just a body. God created you a three-part being, made up of spirit, soul, and body.[12] You're a spirit being with a soul, living in a body.

Fun Fact

The real you isn't defined by your physical body, although that's what's visible. Your spirit and soul—the unseen, non-physical parts of your being—are your true identity markers.

God your Creator is an Intelligent Designer and was very purposeful in the way He created you. Your spirit and soul are the innermost part of your being, designed to fulfill the ultimate divine purpose of God and humanity joined in endless love forever. Sometimes the spirit and soul are mistakenly considered the same, but they're not. They're different and they function differently.

Your spirit bears the stamp of God's Spirit nature or essence, giving you the capacity for a perfectly divine bond of unity with God. Since all humans are created with the same spirit image of God, your spirit is also capable of spirit-to-spirit connections or union with others. Your soul functions as your thinking and decision-making centre through its faculties of mind, emotions, and will. The soul receives impulses from the body through the five physical senses (see, hear, touch, taste, smell) and in turn influences the response of the body. Likewise, God designed the soul to receive divine transmissions from the spirit for expression through the body. The soul is like a "middle-man" that works for the spirit and body. However, because it has the power of free will, the soul can choose to cooperate or not. Like your spirit, your soul is also capable of bonding with others (having soul ties) at an emotional level.

From this brief explanation, you can see the critical part the soul plays in your responses to sexual urges, temptations, and encounters.

Your soul will either side with your body to fulfill its urges or resist the temptations. Whatever you've filled your mind with makes the difference. You'll discover in later chapters that saturating your mind with truths from God's Word, verbal affirmations, and thoughts that reinforce sexual wholeness will strengthen your soul to respond to God's grace and overcome temptations.

So you see, there's more to sexual encounters than what you experience in your body. Hardly anything affects you so greatly at all three levels (spirit, soul, and body) as sexual activities. Why? Because of God's Big Idea in creating sex to be more than a physical act. He designed sex to produce an even greater non-physical union of spirit and soul. Your spirit and soul are actually capable of bonding in far more significant ways than your physical body. That's why words like "fragmentable" and "bondable" are sometimes used to describe certain qualities of the spirit and soul. These words help us understand why even after the body is no longer sexually engaged with someone, or long after a relationship has ended, individuals remain bonded through sexual soul ties.

I'll never forget the response of an older lady when she saw me do a demonstration of sexual bonding. In this demonstration, I tried to rip apart two pieces of cardboard that were strongly glued together. I pulled with great effort, and in the end the separation was messy. Fragments from one piece of the cardboard remained stuck to the other piece. This dear lady could hardly hold the tears back as she said, "No wonder I feel so broken. Parts of me are who knows where. Perhaps even in someone's grave. I want them back." Thankfully, on that day she discovered how to break those soul ties and started her journey of restoration into new dimensions of sexual wholeness.

You'll read more about soul ties later. But for now, let me ask—Do you identify with this woman's need to restore soul fragments because of previous sexual relationships or activities? Don't be dismayed. Soul ties can be broken! The "Sexuality Reset Prayers" in the Bonus Section will help you do just that.

Spiritual Heart

Throughout the book you'll be reading about the heart, or spiritual heart (words used interchangeably), so it's important to have some idea of the meaning. The spiritual heart is another non-physical aspect of your life, which is sometimes thought of as being the same as the soul and spirit. They overlap in some ways, but they're not identical. You're so familiar with technology I know you'll get it right away when I say that your spiritual heart is the "hard drive" of your life. Whatever is consciously or sub-consciously programmed in your heart will come out in various expressions. Feelings, emotions, thoughts, imaginations, and actions originate from what's stored up in the heart. Your passions and affections, for example, reflect your heart. As someone has said, your outside world reflects your inside world.

Your spiritual heart will have a significant effect on your sexual choices, either positively or negatively. Since this is so important, in Chapter 8 you'll be finding out how to nurture your heart to positively influence your pursuit of sexual wholeness.

My parting note in closing out this chapter is that if you identified with the woman's response to my demonstration of sexual bonding, I urge you to head over to the "Sexuality Reset Prayers" after you've completed the chapter reflections.

Chapter 5 Reflections

Did you know?

Sex and nakedness do not equal intimacy.

Words to Live By

"Our bodies are not only biological, they are theological—they tell a divine story." (Christopher West)

Or didn't you realize that your body is a sacred place, the place of the Holy Spirit? Don't you see that you can't live however you please, squandering what God paid such a high price for? The physical part of you is not some piece of property belonging to the spiritual part of you. God owns the whole works. So let people see God in and through your body. (1 Corinthians 6:19–20, The Message)

From Your Heart

Your Affirmation: I joyfully embrace my sexual identity as a gift from God, my Creator and Heavenly Father. I also courageously embrace the changes and feelings in my body as God's design. I ask for and receive strength from God to honour Him with my body and sexual choices.

____

____

____

____

Chapter 6

Big Ideas about Relationship

In this chapter we're going to explore more big ideas from God's original creation designs.

Thanks to scientists like Albert Einstein and Sir Isaac Newton, we've come to recognize and value the scientific laws governing the universe. Laws are simply principles that work the same way, every time, everywhere. The law of gravity is one example.

There are also many spiritual laws or principles of creation that govern our human existence. The laws of love and relationship top the list. The exchange of pure love through relationships is our reason for being—first to experience this kind of relationship between God and ourselves, then with one another.

We don't usually think of love and relationship as laws, but they are. As it is with scientific laws, God created and designed love and relationship to work a certain way. We experience life at its best when we recognize, respect, and cooperate with God's designs, so it's important to know about God's two main relationship models, how they got interrupted, and what God did to restore His intentions for humanity.

Why is this stuff important? Knowing God's thoughts about humanity's relationship with Him is the starting point for understanding your personal and sexual identity. It helps you understand who you are in God's eyes and why He created you male or female. It will also anchor your faith for the pursuit of sexual wholeness, especially if you've had a false start and need to reset.

Two Earthly Relationship Models

In the beginning God designed two earthly relationship models as images of His intended relationship with humanity: The Parent-Child Model and The Husband-Wife Model.

We experience these relationship models in ways that are flawed. But our experiences do not change God's good intentions from the beginning. You may be familiar with the biblical account of creation in the first three chapters of the book of Genesis. A quick review of what the Bible tells us about these two relationship models will be useful because they hold secrets about God's intentions for you and me.

The Parent-Child Model

God created Adam as His son, and they enjoyed close relationship as Father and son in the beginning. The genealogy of Jesus recorded in the Gospel of Luke describes Adam as the son of God. We also know from the creation account that their relationship grew through spirit-to-spirit connections, talking with each other, and being in each other's presence. Adam was an earthly representation of Jesus, the heavenly Son of God. Adam's relationship with God also represented the relationship we're created to have with God as our Heavenly Father.[13]

The Husband-Wife Model

God formed the woman, Eve, from one of Adam's ribs and presented her to him as a perfect companion. The animals that Adam had named and cared for in Eden did not share his God-like nature in the same way, so they couldn't be his companion on an intimate level. When God presented Eve to Adam, he took her as his wife.

The marriage of Adam and Eve, and all earthly marriages, point to the plan God had in mind even before creation. It's the plan to prepare a Bride for His heavenly Son, Jesus Christ. (The Church, made up of the followers of Jesus, is called the Bride of Christ, and the Bible describes this marriage as "The Marriage Supper of the Lamb.")[14]

What Do These Models Say About You?

Here are a few quick points:

- Because the entire human race was created from Adam, it means that you share in all of Adam's experiences.
- The best place to begin your relationship with God is to get to know His heart for you as your loving Heavenly Father.
- The Father desires that you receive and grow in His love as the secure anchor of your life. Believing and trusting in the love that God has for you as a Father gives you deep satisfaction and fulfillment. When you're anchored in your Heavenly Father's love, you're less likely to go looking for love in the wrong places or to mistake sex for love.
- Just as He did in presenting Eve to Adam, your Heavenly Father desires marriage and a "perfect" companion for you. God is a good Father and, like any good earthly father, he wants you to have a marriage that's enriched with sexual wholeness, not shaped by brokenness.
- The Father's good plan is for you to be sexually united as one flesh in a covenant bond of marriage created for the exchange of pure love and intimacy. Genesis 2:25 says, "Adam and his wife were both naked, and they felt no shame." That's because they hadn't experienced sexual brokenness. They were sexually whole. Neither of them had the baggage that comes with false starts and unhealthy sexual soul ties.

Your Sexuality and Faith Aren't Miles Apart

I don't know where you are in your faith journey. Coming to faith in Jesus Christ as your personal Saviour puts you back in relationship with your Heavenly Father as He originally intended. However, even as a follower of Jesus, you may still have some difficulty figuring out how your sexuality and faith journey relate. I wouldn't be surprised if you see them as miles apart or thought you could keep them separate.

That's the way I saw it as a teen and young adult. I thought my sexuality, sexual choices, and faith had nothing to do with each other. As far as I was concerned, the sexual part of my life was my own private business and off limits to God. Wrong! By the time I realized the error in my thinking, I had wandered off course. I'm so grateful that God's grace, mercy, and love are available for resets after a false start. It's never too late to get back on track. And no one is ever too far off track that they can't be restored.

Reset and restoration are certainly possible, but Not Yet! is still the best option. That's why I'm passionate about helping you and other teens find the missing pieces of the puzzle early enough to avoid false starts. That's the purpose of *Ready. Set. Not Yet!* It gives you the missing pieces that I needed as a teenager who loved Jesus and wanted to stay in relationship with Him. I just didn't know how these two seemingly conflicting parts of my life fit together.

"Humpty Dumpty" Had A Great Fall

Remember the Humpty Dumpty nursery rhyme from childhood? It's a great metaphor for the fracturing of humanity's original relationship with God. But unlike the ending of this nursery rhyme, where no one could put Humpty together again, God did put "Humpty" (humanity) back together again.

I won't presume that you know what happened to God's original plan, so I'll provide an overview. It's important to know how God's plans got interrupted and what He did to put things back together. Understanding these truths is important because they explain why there's so much brokenness in the world and why sexual wholeness is such a huge challenge. Above all, knowing what God has done to restore His original design gives you hope for sexual wholeness, even if you've had a false start.

God had instructed Adam not to eat from one of two trees in the centre of the Garden of Eden—the Tree of Knowledge of Good and Evil. I'll refer to it going forward as the Tree of Knowledge. The other tree was the Tree of Life. Adam and Eve were free to eat from the Tree of Life, which would have filled them with more and more of God's life. It would have given them increasing ability to think and choose like God, as well as remain under His protection and provision.

However, Satan disguised himself as a serpent and tempted Eve. She exercised her free will and chose not to follow God's instruction. Both Adam and Eve disregarded the boundary God had established for their benefit and ended up eating from the forbidden tree. Basically, by yielding to Satan's temptation, Adam and Eve chose independence from God's way of life. They chose Satan's way and his nature instead. In this exchange, Adam and Eve received the nature of Satan, which is bent on opposing and rebelling against God's way. This nature is sometimes referred to in the Bible as the "flesh," or the "sin nature."

Adam and Eve sinned by disobeying God and eating from the Tree of Knowledge. Their choice resulted in what's known as the "Fall" of humanity (another way of saying the relationship between God and humanity was broken). The sin nature became the dominant human nature or personality, and rebelling against God became humanity's default. All of us inherited this default from Adam, making it easier to choose our own way independently of God. So don't be surprised that it's going to take intentional effort to wait and observe God's "sex for marriage" design. On the other hand, choosing to satisfy immediate sexual desires will be the easy automatic default.

This choice that Adam and Eve made separated us all from the bond of intimate, loving union we were created to have with God. Our original capacity for the exchange of pure love was severely damaged. We lost the original purity of knowing no shame, and instead a sense of defilement became attached to the human body. In this state of broken relationship with God, the Bible says both Adam and Eve became aware that they were naked. In desperation, they tried using fig leaves to cover their nakedness, and tried to hide from God.[15]

God's love never quits, so He went looking for Adam and Eve, just as He does for all of us. He killed an animal and used its bloody skin to cover their nakedness. The animal slain to provide their covering pointed to Jesus, who is known in the Bible as the Lamb of God slain in eternity (before time began) for the sins of humanity.[16]

"Humpty Dumpty" Got Put Back Together Again

Jesus did put Humpty Dumpty back together again! It's the purpose for which Jesus came to earth. He came to redeem (buy back) and restore all that humanity lost in the "Fall" of Adam and Eve.

Jesus suffered a cruel death on the cross. There He offered His blood as the complete one-time ransom payment for the forgiveness of all of humanity's sins. He took our place—once and for all! The blood of Jesus not only covered our sins, as the blood of the animal did for Adam and Eve, but it put away our sins completely and continues to free us, even today, from the effects of sin. By dying in our place, Jesus made it possible for us to once again experience God's original design—the bond of intimate relationship with Him.

We get put back together again and experience a "reset" when we put our faith in what Jesus did through the cross on our behalf. His righteousness is transferred to us, and we have a "new birth." We're reborn in our spirit by the Spirit of God, not of biological parents as in our natural birth. In the words of the Bible, we become a new creation, fit once again to be the holy habitation for God. *"Therefore, if anyone is in Christ, the new creation has come: The old has gone, the new is here!"*[17]

God is a master at putting people back together

www.christart.com

Now You Know the Rest of The Story

I do hope this chapter connected more dots for you. In the past, your youth leader, a parent, or another adult may have spoken to you about the sin of fornication (the word used in the Bible for sex before marriage). They may have also tried to convince you not to do it because your body is the temple of the Holy Spirit. Perhaps it didn't make sense, or you couldn't figure out why it was such a big deal. Now you know the rest of the story.

From now on, whenever you hear the words "sexual purity," I encourage you to think of the ultimate destiny for which God created you—to share in God's endless, pure love as a majestic, holy habitation for Him. Think sexual wholeness! Remember also that Jesus paid the ransom price of His precious blood on the cross for you to reach that destiny.

There's No Need to Hide From God

Should you miss the mark of God's design for your sexuality, don't try to hide from God like Adam and Eve. God's heart breaks for you, and He wants you to receive His forgiveness and cleansing through the blood of Jesus. Saying a sincere prayer like this one from your heart is all it takes: *Heavenly Father, I'm sorry for making choices contrary to your ways. Please forgive and cleanse me with the blood of Jesus.*

God has lovingly provided practical ways of escape and reset opportunities for you, which you'll find out more about in Section Three. Our next chapter will focus on pursuing sexual wholeness.

Chapter 6 Reflections

Did you know?

When you believe and trust in God's love for you, you're less likely to look for love in the wrong places or mistake sex for love.

Words to Live By

"Because of the forgiving power of Christ, you are a new creation no matter what you've done or where you are." (Jim Burns)

And by the blood of his cross, everything in heaven and earth is brought back to himself—back to its original intent, restored to innocence again! (Colossians 1:20, TPT)

From Your Heart

Your Prayer: I'm grateful for your love, Heavenly Father. Thank you that you loved me too much to leave me separated from you in brokenness and shame. Thank you, Lord Jesus, for your victory on the cross that resets my life and puts me back together. Amen

Chapter 7

Pursuing Sexual Wholeness

Marriage is the "green light" that God has designed for sex. In that respect, marriage is like the final command the sprinter must wait for before leaping from the starting blocks. It's not because God is mean or because He wants to hold out on you that He designed sex for marriage. He just wants the best for you—sexual wholeness.

God designed the covenant of marriage between a man and woman as the environment to safely experience the intimacy you were made for and need. As you would have read in previous chapters, the exchange of love in marriage is an earthly image of the sacred union humanity was created to have with God. Yes, I know. Not all marriages are good or safe, and many even end in divorce. But, in the words of Jesus, "It was not this way from the beginning." The Voice translation says it like this: "Divorce was an innovation, an accommodation to a fallen world. There was no divorce at creation."[18]

The choices that Adam and Eve made really messed up God's original intentions. But in His love for you and me, God paid the ransom price to restore us to wholeness. We don't want to ignore His love gift and continue choosing paths of sexual brokenness.

You'll recall God's instruction to Adam and Eve. They shouldn't eat from the Tree of Knowledge. God knew the outcome. It would've caused them to exchange good for evil and think that what God said wasn't good for them (and us) is "good." By normalizing sexual brokenness, the culture of society has missed it, but you don't have to. Sexual wholeness is possible because God designed you for it and has made provision for you to experience it.

A Big Question

In a panel discussion I led some years ago, a boy in his early teens asked a question that left most of the adults in the room with wide opened mouths. "Is oral sex a sin?" It wasn't the question that shocked them. The shock was who asked the question. They were shocked that someone so young asked the question in such a bold, matter-of-fact way. Yes, was the unanimous response from the panel. Why? Because it's contrary to God's design and purpose for sex. You see, sexual wholeness and purity involve more than abstaining from physical intercourse.

Sexual Workarounds

It was this experience that inspired me to coin the word "workaround" for the various forms of real, virtual, or imagined sexual activities that satisfy immediate sexual desires but deny the greater good for which God designed sex and human sexuality. Workarounds compromise our sexual character and cause sexual brokenness. Unfortunately, it may take a while before we discover what we've done to the sacred image of God that we bear.

Workarounds don't honour you, the other person (real or imagined), or God. It's like purchasing an expensive item on credit—buy now, pay later. Sexual workarounds provide instant gratification, but you pay later in one way or another: emotionally, physically, spiritually. On top of that, you pay with extremely high interest. In Chapter 9 we'll explore some of these "hidden costs," such the effects on one's sense of self worth, brain, and future path in life.

So what will you do with your sexual urges now that you know they aren't green light signals for any kind of sexual workaround? Think about it for a moment because this is a decision you'll be faced with repeatedly.

Why You Shouldn't Do It

Ok. Relax. Breathe. I'm not about to give you a long list of risks associated with pre-marital sex or other workarounds. You're probably already quite familiar with these risks. If you aren't, there are many good resources online based on biblical truths that will bring you up to speed.

I once heard someone say that teenagers are risk-takers and that trying to scare them with the risks of pre-marital sex isn't going to stop them. Just in case you're wondering why this is so, it has to do with how the brain develops.

Brainy Fun Fact

The rational, decision-making part of your brain (the prefrontal cortex) isn't fully developed. That doesn't happen until you're in your mid-twenties.[19]

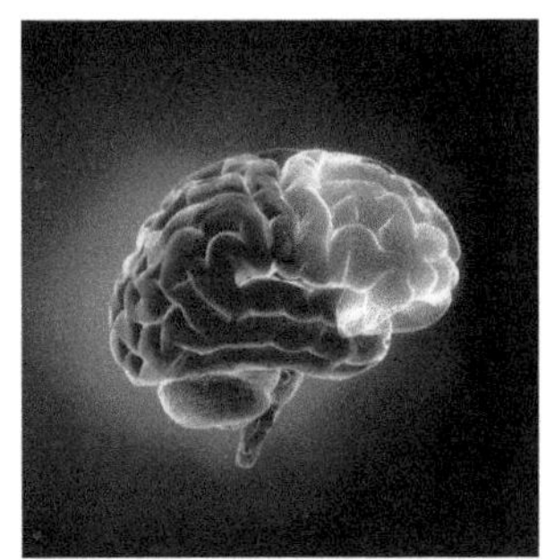

Motivating Examples of Sexual Wholeness

I understand that telling you about the risks of pre-marital sex may not be a strong enough motivation to stop you from doing it. So instead of a list of risks, I have three examples that will hopefully motivate you to focus on the world of possibilities (the good things) available to you when you pursue sexual wholeness.

1. **The Olympic sprinter: An icon of self-control and patience**

   This first example reminds you that an Olympic sprinter in the starting blocks perfectly represents your pursuit of sexual wholeness. You know the three starting commands: Ready. Set. Go! After the second command, the sprinter must override the urge to go and patiently wait for the final command. A false start will result in disqualification. The possibility of winning a medal will be lost.

   You deserve the best God has for you—the gold medal of sexual wholeness! So keep your feet grounded in those blocks in the *Not Yet!* zone. Exercise the self-control and patience that's characteristic of champion athletes. Wait to run your sexual race in God's way according to His design in marriage.

2. **Daniel and his three friends: An icon of determination and courage**

   There's a story in the Bible from the book of Daniel about four brilliant Hebrew teenagers who were exiled to Babylon and plunged into an ungodly culture. What these young men faced wasn't unlike the challenges you face in today's sex-saturated culture. The king expected them to embrace the Babylonian way of life. The Bible says this about Daniel's response to the king's plan: "But Daniel purposed in his heart that he would not defile himself."[20]

   Daniel's friends shared his determination. All three of them set their hearts to honour God no matter what. You'll also have to decide—not in your head but in your heart—not to compromise the sacredness of your body with sexual workarounds. While in the *Not Yet!* zone, with your heart set on God, you stand a better chance of not yielding to temptation when it comes.

When Daniel's three friends refused to worship a Babylonian statue, the king had them thrown into a fiery furnace. But God stood with them in the fire, and they came out unharmed. In the end, because of their faith and courage, they received a promotion, and the king acknowledged their God as the true God.

Choosing to honour God in your sexuality instead of doing what is popular in the culture around you may sometimes feel like you're in a fiery furnace. God made a way of escape for these three teenagers, and He will for you as well. Even more, God will honour you for honouring him, and promotion will come to you. In other words, honouring God in your sexuality sets you up to receive His very best.

**3. Mary the teenage virgin:
An icon of sexual wholeness and purity**

Mary, the virgin girl who became the mother of Jesus, was about fourteen years old when the angel visited her and revealed God's plan. The angel announced to her that she had found favour with God, and He had chosen her to be the mother of His Son, Jesus.

Being a virgin, Mary asked how this would happen. The angel told her: "The Holy Spirit will come upon you, and the power of the Most High will overshadow you. So the baby to be born will be holy, and he will be called the Son of God."[21]

Long before, an Old Testament prophet, Isaiah, had told the people that God would give them a sign. "A virgin shall conceive and give birth to a son who would be called Immanuel, meaning God with us."[22] Mary was that "sign." To understand the mystery of this sign, think back to the ten *Big Ideas* you read in Chapter 5. Mary's conception by the Holy Spirit is an icon of God's ultimate creation plan for humanity to be His habitation. Mary's virginity represented the purity that is essential for such a habitation. Because of her sexual wholeness and willingness to give herself to God for His purpose, she experienced the greatest honour and privilege known to humanity.

Take that in for a minute. A virgin teenager birthed the Holy Son of God! That was a one-time privilege. However, God's desire for you, me, and all of humanity is for us to receive and bring forth His Spirit, which is the Spirit of Holiness. So don't get frustrated the next time someone encourages you to pursue holiness and purity. It's an encouragement to pursue sexual wholeness.

You may not have understood this before, but now you do. See it as an opportunity for God to conceive and bring forth something of Himself and His divine purpose from you. Why would you turn down such a privilege?

Word Gem

Sexual purity is a powerful icon pointing to the Holy God having an earthly temple that is fit for Him to inhabit.

Present-Day Marys and Daniels

It's good for you to know that there are present-day Marys and Daniels in your generation. They have embraced the privilege of honouring God with their sexuality. The instruction they receive about God's divine purpose for sex (much like what you're getting here), and the support of godly mentors is helping them to stay focused. Similar to the vision that champion athletes have, they carry on the inside a mental picture of their God-designed future. The passion to discover and fulfill the life of significance for which they're born empowers them to resist the pressure of the culture around them. As a wise young man said to me, "It may look that way, but not all teenagers are having sex."

You Have What It Takes

You may be thinking that choosing and pursuing the path of sexual wholeness is easier said than done. You're right. It's not easy. But here's a promise from God to you: The Lord says, "I will guide you along the best pathway for your life. I will advise you and watch over you."[23] The Lord always keeps His promise!

Mary and the three Hebrew young men didn't fulfill God's plan in their own strength. Neither do today's young people who are committed to saving sex for marriage. God's enabling power (His grace) works in them and helps them to overcome every temptation. This same grace is also available to you. You have what it takes to resist sexual workarounds and experience sexual wholeness!

I wrote this book because I believe that when you understand the spiritual mysteries about sex and human sexuality, you're better prepared to choose the path of sexual wholeness. One of those mysteries or secrets you need to be aware of is that your pursuit of sexual wholeness involves a spiritual battle. That's the topic of our next chapter.

Chapter 7 Reflections

Did you know? While the pre-frontal cortex of your brain is still developing, there are ways to make wise, rational choices. You can ask for the help of the Holy Spirit, follow godly instruction, and stay accountable to adults who have your best interest at heart.

Words to Live By "Purity of life is not a quest for perfection as much as it is a quest for liberation from those things that may inhibit effectiveness and reduce power-filled living." (Jack Hayford)

"There is no greater privilege than being a host to God Himself." (Bill & Beni Johnson)

From Your Heart **Your Prayer:** Heavenly Father, in the Name of Jesus, I ask for courage and determination to guard my heart. Help me to be diligent in reading and meditating on your words of wisdom instead of filling my mind with sexual thoughts and images. Amen.

____

____

____

____

____

____

Chapter 8

You're in a Battle

What you don't know will hurt you. That's why it's critical for you to be aware, sooner rather than later, that your sexuality is at the centre of a fierce invisible battle. Your thoughts are very important in this battle, so this chapter includes strategies for dealing with your thoughts.

The COVID-19 (Coronavirus) pandemic that brought the world to a screeching halt in 2020 is a perfect illustration of the invisible battle you're in. The expression "invisible enemy" was among the top trending words as cases and deaths skyrocketed. Broadcasters said it repeatedly: "We're at war, fighting an invisible battle against an invisible enemy." Is it really possible for an invisible enemy and an invisible battle to cause as much havoc as the Coronavirus did? Yes! Invisible battles do have devastating consequences.

Understanding Your Battle

The better equipped you are for this battle, the greater your odds of winning. You need answers for these important questions:

1. Who is behind this battle?
2. What kind of battle is it?
3. What is at stake in this battle?

4. Where is the battleground?
5. Why is the battle taking place?

Question #1: Who is behind this battle?

Satan is God's enemy, and he's yours too. He resents God's intentions for creating humans as a dwelling place for His Spirit and to represent Him in the earth. Satan's strategy hasn't changed since the Garden of Eden. He knows that he's no match for God, so he works through us to sabotage God's purposes.

Word Gem

This is not a wrestling match against a human opponent. We are wrestling with rulers, authorities, the powers who govern this world of darkness, and spiritual forces that control evil in the heavenly world.

Ephesians 6:12, GW

Question #2: What kind of battle is it?

The battle is spiritual, so it's important that you understand your spiritual identity. As you would have read in Chapter 5, God created you in His Spirit image to share His Spirit essence. That means you're first and foremost a spiritual being. God also designed your spiritual essence to be expressed through your soul and through your physical body with its male or female differentiations. You are a spiritual being living in a human body with sexual characteristics.

Question #3: What is at stake in this battle?

Your sexuality is the treasure that's at stake in this battle. Here's a quote that I'd like you to read a few times: "*If you want to know what is most sacred in the world, all we need to do is look for what is most violently profaned.*" The author, Christopher West, is talking about sex.[24]

Satan knows that your body, sex, and your sexuality are sacred. The motive behind his temptations is to get you to violate God's design for your body. He wants you to compromise its sacredness by engaging in sexual activities as you please. Your sexuality is at the centre of this spiritual contest because whoever or whatever has power over your sexuality controls your choices and ultimately your destiny. Your sexual choices have a ripple effect on everything—the expression of your true spirituality, your relationships, the fulfillment of your life's purpose, your influence on future generations, and your eternal destiny.

Question #4: Where is the battleground

The battleground is your mind, which is a faculty of your soul. Sexual desires aren't purely physical. The thoughts of your mind are the control centre for the sexual urges you feel in your body. By developing the discipline of self-control in your thought life, you'll master the sexual urges in your body. As someone rightly said, "*Where the mind goes the body follows.*"

Question #5: Why is the battle taking place?

These four points sum up what Satan wants to accomplish through his violent battle against your sexuality.

1. To get you to live as though there's nothing more to your existence than your body and its sexual feelings.
2. To get you to reject God's design and standards and make choices that aren't God-approved. Ultimately this battle is a kingdom clash. When you reject God's standards for human

sexuality, you're siding with Satan and representing his kingdom instead of God's. When Daniel and his three friends faced a kingdom clash in Babylon, they sided with God.

3. To get you to interrupt God's timetable for your life and throw the rhythm of your whole life out of sync. When your life is off balance, among other losses, you end up with detours, unnecessary delays, misdirected energy, emotional pain, and wasted potential.
4. To get you to trade your greatness (God-given treasures and purpose) for counterfeit, short-lived pleasures.

Thoughts Are a Spiritual Weapon

Since the battle is spiritual, the weapons used in the battle also must be spiritual. Thoughts are the number one spiritual weapon Satan uses against you because of how powerful thoughts are. He knows that your actions eventually follow the direction of your thoughts.

Here are a few important things to know about thoughts:

Thoughts register in your mind but originate in your spiritual heart (mostly from what's hidden in your subconscious).

Thoughts are inspired mainly by three sources.

1. God (including what the Bible says, the influence of the Holy Spirit, and God's angel messengers).
2. Satan (including his messengers and influence on social culture).
3. Yourself (including the totality of your past experiences, the influence of family, peers, culture, and the beliefs you internalize).

Battle Strategies

Each of the above sources has a battle strategy.

God's Strategy

The Passion Translation of 2 Corinthians 10:3–5 gives a great description of God's battle strategy: "*For although we live in the natural realm, we don't wage a military campaign employing human weapons...our spiritual weapons are energized with divine power...We capture, like prisoners of war, every thought and insist that it bow in obedience to the Anointed One.*" (Christ, the Anointed One, is the title or name that captures the identity of Jesus as the Messiah chosen by God).

To benefit from God's battle strategy, you need to have a personal relationship with Jesus. It also requires that you know what the Word of God says about the way God sees you and your sexuality.

Satan's Strategy

Satan's strategy is to hijack, defile, twist, and pollute your mind with his thoughts, then to deceive you into believing that they're your own. He even knows how to generate unhealthy thoughts from your past experiences.

His thoughts come in the form of temptations and lies, such as: everyone is doing it; you'll feel so much better; or God is old-fashioned. Once you believe and accept his lies, you naturally proceed to act on them.

Sexual temptation is a spiritual (unseen) bully, and you need a spiritual strategy to overcome Satan's bullying.

Your Strategy

Your strategy is to discern the influence behind each thought and capture those that contradict God's design for sex and your sexuality. When you capture thoughts, you subdue, demolish, and remove them.

It's important to replace unhealthy thoughts with healthy ones, and to replace lies with God's truth.

You fill your mind with God's Word and bombard undesirable thoughts with truth from His Word. (Jesus overcame the temptations of Satan in the wilderness by speaking God's Word).

The ABC of How to Arm Your Thinking

Defensively, you capture thoughts. Offensively, you arm your thinking.

Have you ever seen news reports of how people batten down everything and prepare their homes for a hurricane? They bolt, fasten, and secure all the vulnerable points. Well, preparing your mind for sexual temptation is somewhat like that.

Story Bite

In my first year of high school, someone told me that I wasn't a man until I had sex. Now as a young adult, I realized he was so wrong. I wish I hadn't listened to his bad advice. I paid for it in many ways.

—Tyrone

To arm your thinking means being proactive in renewing and preparing your mind before temptation comes. That way you build up insulation to keep out unhealthy influences from friends, social media, music, movies, and other sources. You also build up resistance to unhealthy thoughts. Should any sneak in, they have no chance of dominating your mind. The more you arm your thinking, the more effective you'll be at overcoming sexual temptation.

Here's your ABC battle strategy:

A. Choose sides. Decide in your heart whose side you're on. Choose God's side each morning you wake up and every time you face a sexual temptation. Daniel and his friends made the choice to not defile themselves right from the start of their exile into the Babylonian culture that was hostile to God. As it was for Daniel and his friends, surrounding yourself with like-minded peers will also reinforce your choice to honour God in your thought life and actions.

B. Purify your heart. You'll recall the metaphor of your spiritual heart being the "hard drive" of your life. Whatever is programmed there will overflow into your thoughts, either positively or negatively. For your thoughts and actions to be pure, your heart must be pure, as these Bible verses reveal:

- "Guard your heart above all else, for it determines the course of your life." [25]
- "For it is from within, out of a person's heart, that evil thoughts come—sexual immorality ..." [26]
- "Cleanse your heart, because your mind is split down the middle, your love for God on one side and selfish pursuits on the other." [27]

Sexual wholeness starts with the heart and thoughts. That's why in Psalm 51, after committing the sin of adultery, King David cried out to God for a "pure heart." Psalm 51 is a perfect prayer-psalm to keep in your collection of spiritual weapons.

C. Fill up on God's Word. A heart that is filled with God's pure Word is a pure heart. You fill up your heart by reading, meditating on what you read, and by memorization. Here's the benefit from Psalm 119:11, plain and simple— *"I have hidden your word in my heart, that I might not sin against you."*

I still have an old, tattered Bible from my teen years. I had written this inscription at the front: *"This book will keep me from sin, or sin will keep me from it."* Regrettably, in some of the early seasons of my life, the latter proved to be true. I missed it, but you don't have to.

Story Bite

I regret not taking the book of Proverbs seriously as a youth. If I had read it daily, the way I now do as an adult, the wisdom would have prepared me to fight my sexual temptations and wait until marriage to have sex.

—Angela

Being Battle Ready

When you arm your thinking, you become battle ready. Then, when you're tempted to act on the sexual urges you feel in your body, you take control of your thoughts and mind. The Holy Spirit helps you to take the Word of God that is hidden in your heart and use it as a razor-sharp spiritual sword against these tempting thoughts.

When dealing with sexual temptations, it may be easy to think that if you could only get your mind to stop thinking sexual thoughts, you'd be okay. That's not actually true, and to some extent may not even be possible. God created you a male or female sexual being with urges, feelings, and thoughts. (As you now know, they have deeper meanings and are designed to be fulfilled in marriage). What matters most is what you do with those thoughts. Repressing them doesn't work. Neither can you ignore them. And you definitely don't want to indulge. You're in a spiritual battle, so your surest path to victory is to use your spiritual battle strategy.

God has made a way of escape for you in every temptation you face. That's such great news! I've dedicated a whole chapter in the next section to your way of escape.

Chosen to Come Alongside You

I'm inviting you to celebrate the awesomeness of God with me for a moment. Long before you came into being, God had you in mind and chose me to come alongside you in this spiritual battle for your sexuality. For some "unknown" reason, my parents gave me the middle name Militia. "What on earth were your parents thinking when they gave you this name?" I was totally embarrassed when my first-year Social Science professor blurted out that question during her first attendance check. I could have strangled her. The lecture hall was filled with over two hundred students. Mark you, it was a good question because I had asked it many times myself. It just wasn't the place to ask it.

But really, why would they have given me a name that has to do with fighting battles? The reserve army of a nation made up of regular citizens trained for emergency service is called the militia. As you can imagine, I hated the name. Not anymore, though! I've since come to realize that it's a perfect fit for my calling to be a spiritual advocate for young people like you. There's a cause, and they named me Militia for such a time as this!

Chapter 8 Reflections

Did you know?	Once you develop the discipline of self-control in your thought life, the results will show up in your body.
Words to Live By	Create a new, clean heart within me. Fill me with pure thoughts and holy desires, ready to please you. (Psalm 51:10, TPT) "Every battle is won or lost in the arena of your mind." (Cindy Trimm) "When you change your thoughts, you will change your feelings as well, and you will also eliminate the triggers that set off those feelings." (Michele Goldstein)
From Your Heart	**Your Affirmation:** I say in faith that my thoughts, words, and actions are moving in the right direction because I read, rehearse, and fill my heart with the truth and wisdom of God's Word. With the help of the Holy Spirit, I daily arm my thinking and win this spiritual battle over my sexuality.

Chapter 9

False Starts Are Costly

If there's a single lesson you've learned from the sprinters at the start of a race and the children in the marshmallow experiment, it's that false starts are costly. The same is true for you concerning sexual activities in the *Not Yet!* zone. Earlier I said that I wouldn't give you a list of the risks associated with pre-marital sex. I'm keeping my promise. Here's what I'll do instead. As we wrap up this section, I'll share with you some of the lesser-known implications of sexual workarounds.

The cultural perspective is that sexual encounters before marriage are a personal and private matter, and that you can get around the consequences by having safe sex. But that's not entirely true. As you now know, *"sex is as much spiritual mystery as physical fact,"*[28] so safe sex won't protect you from some consequences. Based on the spiritual mysteries you read about in earlier chapters, using sex and your sexuality in ways God didn't intend does result in different forms of sexual brokenness. Your spiritual and emotional wellbeing, your brain health, and your life's purpose are some of the main areas affected.

As you read about these implications of sexual brokenness, keep in mind that God in His love has made provision for you to reset and get back on the path of sexual wholeness. We've touched on this in previous chapters, but you'll find lots more in the next section—"Reset and Reroute."

Your Spiritual Wellbeing

Your main identity definition is that you are a spiritual being. It follows that just about everything you do affects your spiritual health either directly or indirectly. In creating you, God shared His Spirit essence with you so that you can enjoy a close, heart-to-heart relationship with Him. Using sex and your sexuality in ways God did not intend compromises your relationship with Him. It also creates unhealthy spiritual bonds with others.

- The first humans, Adam and Eve, hid from God after they sided with Satan. A similar thing will happen in your relationship with God when you're making choices that you know are displeasing to Him. (I know this firsthand!)
- The magnificent opportunity you have for God to bring forth something of Himself from your life gets put on hold. As you'll recall about Mary, the mother of Jesus and the ultimate icon of sexual wholeness, God's desire is also for you to receive and express the life of His pure Holy Spirit.
- Having sex causes you to unite with the other person in a spiritual bond (one flesh union or soul tie). God designed this kind of bonding to occur in the safe environment of a permanent marriage covenant. The soul ties created by sexual relations before marriage can be very damaging, especially because these relationships are often temporary.

Your Emotional (Psychological) Wellbeing

Studies have shown that many sexually active teens, especially girls, experience feelings of shame, anger, regret, self loathing, and worthlessness. They're also more likely to experience depression and suicidal thoughts.

- The soul ties that develop from sexual activities before marriage set you up for heartbreak when the sexual partner "moves on." Oxytocin is the bonding chemical, and it has greater effects in females. Girls suffer longer and harder from breakups for this reason.
- It gets even more complicated when the abortion of an unwanted pregnancy is involved. Some of the emotional consequences may show up right away. Others may take a while. The lingering effects can have a negative impact on your life and marriage. Abortions also affect guys, as many do struggle with guilt afterwards.
- The spiritual and psychological attachments to previous sexual partners don't vanish after getting married. They carry over and will interfere with your marriage relationship.

Your Brain Health

Different areas of your brain regulate different activities. The limbic system is the part of your brain that's given to impulsive responses or instant gratification. Another part, the prefrontal cortex, also known as the executive centre or rational part of the brain, promotes self-control and delayed gratification.[29]

- When you instantly gratify the sexual desires God designed in your body, instead of waiting until marriage, you affect the structure and chemistry of your brain. Your brain gets thrown into an abnormal state. (Porn use, for example, causes the secretion of unnaturally high levels of the chemical dopamine in the brain, which leads to other health issues).
- Repeated actions that respond to the impulsive part of the brain train and strengthen that part. Inadvertently, you end up stifling the growth of the executive or rational decision-making centre of your brain. This can affect your progress in other areas of life

once your brain is trained to the instant gratification default instead of discipline and self-control.[30]

Your Life's Purpose

Your existence isn't accidental. God created you to fulfill a unique purpose. You are His choice and solution for a specific need in your generation and those to come. I find Jeremiah 1:5 quite fascinating. In this verse God told the prophet Jeremiah that He knew him before He formed him in his mother's womb. He also told Jeremiah that He had set him apart for a particular purpose before he was born. This truth isn't about Jeremiah only. It's about you as well. Another amazing verse is Psalm 139:16, which tells us that God has a book of destiny in which He has laid out His good plans for each of our lives. He wrote these plans even before the first day of our lives. The Bible also says, "For we are God's masterpiece. He has created us anew in Christ Jesus, so we can do the good things he planned for us long ago."[31]

- The spiritual, emotional, and physical effects of sexual workarounds will directly or indirectly affect your ability to discover, pursue, and fulfill the purpose for which God chose you. It was marked out just for you before you were even conceived in your mother's womb.
- God has a season and a time planned for every aspect of your life, and He makes everything beautiful in its time.[32] Sexual workarounds compromise God's timetable. An interruption of God's timing in one area of life can throw off the timing in others and have unfavourable implications.
- Because of sexual brokenness, you may experience delays and setbacks in achieving your dreams and goals. Without a reset, you could even miss your destiny and the fulfillment that comes from making a difference in this world. When sex is abused (not experienced God's way) it can be a destiny thief.

What Satan Leaves Out

I was preparing to write this chapter when I heard Pastor Steven Furtick of Elevation Church make a point in one of his messages that perfectly echoes what this chapter is all about: "When the devil tempts you, he leaves a lot of stuff out about what it's going to cost you."

Satan leaves out the hidden costs of sexual workarounds. But you now know what some of those are!

If you've come to the end of this chapter wishing that you could turn back the hands of time, take a deep breath! God has a plan, and there's hope!

Chapter 9 Reflections

Did you know?	The concept of "safe sex" before marriage is an illusion because there are many hidden costs.
Words to Live By	The thief's purpose is to steal and kill and destroy. My purpose is to give them a rich and satisfying life. (John 10:10, NLT) Run from sexual sin! No other sin so clearly affects the body as this one does. For sexual immorality is a sin against your own body. (1 Corinthians 6:18, NLT)
From Your Heart	**Your Prayer:** Thank you, Heavenly Father, for giving me the wisdom, knowledge, and understanding I need to make wise sexual choices for my total wellbeing. When I'm tempted to make unhealthy choices, I ask you to please remind me of the many hidden costs of sexual brokenness. I ask this in the Name of Jesus. Amen.

Section 2 Take-Aways

The Main Thing

Read these key points from the section and circle a number from 1–5 to indicate how much you have embraced each truth. *("1" is "I totally disagree" and "5" is "I agree completely.")*

Highlight the key points with a score of 3 or less and make them the focus of your prayer practice below.

The sexual urges in my body are part of God's design. They're icons for greater spiritual and relational needs.

1 2 3 4 5

God made my body for the grand purpose of being the majestic, holy habitation of His Spirit now and for eternity.

1 2 3 4 5

I am a spirit being with a soul living in a human body that has sexual characteristics.

1 2 3 4 5

My sexuality cannot be separated from God.

1 2 3 4 5

I'll experience my best life by cooperating with God's designs for love, relationship, sex, and marriage.

1 2 3 4 5

The Main Thing (cont'd)

Because of what Jesus did to restore God's original design for human sexuality, I can experience sexual wholeness even after a false start.

1 2 3 4 5

My sexuality is at the centre of a fierce, invisible, spiritual battle, because whoever or whatever has power over my sexuality controls my choices and ultimately my destiny.

1 2 3 4 5

I have what it takes to resist sexual workarounds and pursue sexual wholeness.

1 2 3 4 5

I must first develop the discipline of self-control in my thought life, then the results will show up in my body. My thoughts are the control centre of sexual urges.

1 2 3 4 5

The concept of safe sex before marriage is an illusion because there are many hidden costs.

1 2 3 4 5

Prayer Practice

Speak to your Heavenly Father and ask Him to help you with the key points above that you need to internalize more fully. You may wish to write your prayer, and remember to include anyone who may be having similar challenges.

____

____

____

____

____

____

____

____

____

____

____

____

____

____

Your Call to Action

Identify at least one action you're committed to taking based on something you discovered in this section. Remember to use your "memory tools."

____

____

____

____

____

____

____

A Blessing

Beloved teen, I bless you with awareness that it's the power of God working in you that enables you to overcome temptations. May you not rely on your own strength to win but learn instead to draw on God's power. May you fill your heart with words of wisdom and pray to strengthen your mind where temptations begin. I bless you to be honest about your weaknesses and to be accountable to mentors for support. You're blessed in the Name of the Lord. (Bite-Size Blessing Power Edition: Overcoming Temptations)

Section 3

Reset and Reroute

Chapter 10

Reset Is Possible

You've come to my favourite chapter in the whole book! It will likely be yours too once you're done.

If you've jumped the gun and had a false start, I've got great news for you: God doesn't have a "one-false-start" rule! Usain Bolt was disqualified from the 100-metre race, but you can get back into the starting blocks and start over as if you hadn't false started.

And if you gave in and ate the marshmallow, it's not too late to start building the discipline of self-control before the next marshmallow test rolls around. Oh, yes! There will be many more tests and many more opportunities to develop the discipline to wait. Each time you wait, your self-control muscles get stronger and stronger.

It's never too late to experience sexual wholeness! Ultimately, it's about the moment-by-moment choices you make, regardless of previous unhealthy choices. Here's something I remind myself about again and again: "God loves me too much to leave me the way I am." It's my memorial of faith, hope, grace, and gratitude that I return to, especially when I've messed up (missed God's mark or violated His way, AKA sinned).

Our loving Heavenly Father seeks out you and me just as He did when He went looking for Adam and Eve in Eden and covered their shame. Think back for a moment to what you read about their experience in Chapter 6. The bloody skin of the animal God used to cover them was a picture of the blood of Jesus, which paid in full for every one of our violations against God.

The Grace Exchange

The trading floors of the stock exchanges around the world buzz with action when they're open for business. Well, God also has a trading floor that I call the Grace Exchange. It's open 24/7! You and I have the privilege of stepping onto God's trading floor at any time to "trade" with the blood of Jesus. It's not complicated at all. We go there with complete assurance that Jesus paid in full for all our sins. We can, therefore, be confident that God will not remember our past once we sincerely acknowledge what we've done, have a change of heart (that's what repentance is), and receive His forgiveness through the blood of Jesus.

God has a special place in this heavenly trading floor called the Throne of Grace.[33] I often think of Him sitting there graciously waiting with His hand poised over the reset button. He gives an open invitation for you to come and trade in your past for the new beginning that Jesus purchased for you on the cross with His precious blood.

If you know about the factory reset of a Nintendo system or iPhone, then you understand what I mean. The old data is permanently deleted, the system is restored to original factory settings, and it starts to run like new.

The Ultimate Reset

I found language in The Passion Translation of the Bible that perfectly describes the comprehensive, all-inclusive reset that the Heavenly Father accomplished on our behalf through the blood of Jesus.

The verse is posted on my wall and forever tattooed on my heart. Colossians 1:20 is what I call the ultimate reset!

Word Gem

And by the blood of his cross, everything in heaven and earth is brought back to himself—back to its original intent, restored to innocence again!

Colossians 1:20, TPT

How To Have a Personal Reset

This is your opportunity if you haven't yet personally put your faith in what Jesus did at the cross for you. As you would have read earlier, we all shared in Adam and Eve's experience and became like Humpty Dumpty. In addition to the legacy of sin inherited from Adam and Eve, we've also made our own choices that placed us at odds with God and left us desperately in need of a personal reset.

Jesus poured out His life blood on the cross and paid in full for us to be put back together again. The Father raised Jesus from the dead so that by faith in Him you can have new spiritual life. Jesus is the only One who makes a complete reset possible.

There are two simple steps to a complete personal reset.

1. Believe in your heart that Jesus died for you.
2. Confirm your faith with your words.

This simple prayer in the text box will help you to do that.

> *Dear Jesus, I ask you to reset my life. I'm sorry for going against God's way. Thank you for dying on the cross for me. I now choose to follow you as my Saviour and Lord. I open the door of my heart and receive you now. Thank you for the gift of forgiveness, for my new life, and for the relationship that I now share with you, the Father and the Holy Spirit. Amen.*

It's done! You said that prayer in faith, and an instant spiritual transaction occurred. You have a new beginning even if you don't feel any different. The Father wiped your slate completely clean with the blood of Jesus. Every violation against God has been removed, and you are free from them.

Welcome to your clean, new slate!

Your Sexuality Reset

I don't know what your sexual journey has been like so far. Have you had a false start and feel it was so bad that you need more help to get over it? If that's the case, I encourage you to share your struggles with your pastor, a mentor, a professional counsellor, or your parents. The most important thing is to run to God instead of hiding. Talk to your Heavenly Father about what you're struggling with, ask for the cleansing power of the blood of Jesus to wash you, and rest in His loving, healing embrace. Adam and Eve made the mistake of trying to hide, but you don't have to.

And don't stop praying!

In one of my focus groups with teens and young adults, I shared copies of prayers I had written for sexual wholeness. When they read the prayers, a few attendees responded as if I'd given them a million dollars. I've included sexuality reset prayers in the Bonus Section because I understand how difficult it is to come up with words to express what you really want to say in prayer. But may I encourage you to go to your Heavenly Father and just talk. Remember that prayer is having conversation with Him, just as you'd talk with another person. Don't overthink it. He's so merciful and kind. Don't forget the love He demonstrated to Adam and Eve when He found them hiding. He didn't scold or reprimand them. Instead, He overwhelmed them with a generous dose of His loving grace.

This Thing Called Grace

I've come across folks who are afraid of grace. They think that young people will abuse grace—taking it as permission to do things that displease God because they know they'll be forgiven. But that's not what God's grace is all about.

Word Gem

The grace of God enables you to do what you cannot do in your own strength.

Grace is the undeserved favour of God that equips you with power to live free from anything that opposes His intentions for your life. Because of His love for you, your Heavenly Father lavishes His grace upon you to work in your heart and empower you day by day. Grace is what enables you to experience the intimate heart-to-heart relationship with God for which you were made. That's why Jesus came to the earth "full of grace and truth."[34] And that's also why the Father's heavenly throne is called the Throne of Grace.

With His blood, Jesus paid in full for you to experience the fullness of God's grace in every area of your life, including your sexuality. When you receive God's provision of abundant grace, the sin of sexual brokenness will not dominate your life. The Bible assures you that instead you will reign over sin through Christ Jesus.[35]

Your Grace Pathway

In your pursuit of sexual wholeness, you'll likely feel frustrated unless you fully embrace God's pathway of grace. Grace meets you where you're at. Your commitment to sexual wholeness doesn't mean that you're never going to mess things up. Neither does it mean you're a failure if you do. Just know that grace will always meet you exactly where you are, once you choose to agree with God's design for sex and sexuality. Your focus isn't on whether you can keep the commitment. Your focus is on the grace of God that will fully guard every stage of your journey.

Extreme Grace in Action

Did you know that the Bible includes many examples of grace for sexuality reset? It's true that the fullness of grace came through Jesus. But even prior to this, we have in the Old Testament what I call extreme grace in action. Let me share a few examples with you.[36]

- The ancestry of Jesus included three women with sexual brokenness in their personal or family history—Rahab, Ruth, and Tamar. Rahab was a prostitute. Ruth had a family lineage of incest. Tamar became pregnant by disguising herself as a prostitute to seduce her father-in-law.

- King David also features prominently in the genealogy of Jesus, yet he had committed adultery and arranged for the woman's husband to be killed in battle.

Imagine that! What point is God making by including individuals with such sexual brokenness in the human ancestry of His Son, Jesus? Don't miss this—God can and will redeem (reset) the most broken past and use it for His purpose.

No matter where you've been, you're not disqualified. Hebrews 8:12 tells you why: *"For I will be merciful to their unrighteousness, and their sins and their lawless deeds I will remember no more."* Beloved teen, may you always find hope in God's fountain of grace and mercy!

These are amazing examples of what the Bible means when it says we're justified by grace, through faith, by the blood of Jesus.[37] The word "justified" basically means "just as if you had not." It holds the secret to experiencing a sexuality reset. You need to see this as the expression of God's extravagant love. It repositions you where God intended you to be, regardless of where you've been.

What If You Need a Reset Because of What Someone Did?

I'm fully aware of the possibility that your sexuality may need a reset because of what someone else did to you (molestation or rape). If that's the case, I'm truly sorry.

I like these four points that author Jim Burns says anyone who has been sexually abused must hear:

1. It's not your fault.
2. Seek help. Don't suffer in silence.
3. There is hope (for your future).

4. God cares. He really does.[38]

On behalf of the person or persons who abused you, I ask for your forgiveness. I know it's not easy to forgive someone who has hurt you so badly, but it's your pathway to full and complete freedom. I'm also asking our Heavenly Father to give you His supernatural strength (grace) to do through you what you can't do on your own.

Please know that there's power in the blood of Jesus to heal you completely (spiritually, emotionally, mentally, and physically). Right now you can receive a reset and be made whole in every part.

Granting forgiveness to your abuser(s) doesn't let them off the hook. Rather, it opens the cage in which you've been locked up with them.

Forgiveness releases YOU!

Would you take a moment to open that cage in prayer? As you begin to pray, I want you to feel the comforting embrace of your loving Heavenly Father as His love washes over you, and His blood cleanses you.

Heavenly Father, I receive your supernatural strength, and choose to forgive __________ (insert names) for the pain they've caused me. I now receive from you the full reset of my sexuality in the places that were broken by these experiences. I receive your complete cleansing by the blood of Jesus. Thank you for my total freedom from every lingering trace of pain, guilt, shame, loss, and trauma. Restore your peace and wholeness where there has been turmoil in my sexuality. I pray this in the Name of Jesus. Amen

Your prayer of faith has set you free, healed, and cleansed you! The healing you receive may take time to show up in your feelings, thoughts, and emotions. I encourage you to reach for support when you need it, especially from someone who is a trained specialist in trauma resolution.

Now let me speak words of blessing over you that will impart the supernatural power of God into your life. The blessing you're about to receive is from the book of Genesis and is based on the names of two boys: Manasseh (meaning to make forgetful) and Ephraim (meaning to make fruitful and prosperous).[39]

My beloved teen, I deposit this blessing by faith into the depths of your spirit and into every broken place. May God make you like Ephraim and Manasseh. May His supernatural presence and power in your life cause you to forget the pain of the past. And may He make you fruitful and prosperous in the future. You're blessed in the Name of the Lord.

This is a good place to linger for a few moments and let that blessing sink in.

The Touch of The Master's Hand

We'll wrap up this chapter with a poem that has been a great source of inspiration, encouragement and hope for me at various stages of my journey. I'm sharing this poem about a broken violin with you because it's an excellent metaphor of sexuality reset.

THE OLD VIOLIN

THE TOUCH OF THE MASTER'S HAND

> 'Twas battered and scarred,
> And the auctioneer thought it
> hardly worth his while
> To waste his time on the old violin,
> but he held it up with a smile.
>
> "What am I bid, good people," he cried,
> "Who starts the bidding for me?
> "One dollar, one dollar, Do I hear two?
> "Two dollars, who makes it three?
> "Three dollars once, three dollars twice, going for three."
>
> But, no,
> From the room far back a gray bearded man
> Came forward and picked up the bow,
> Then wiping the dust from the old violin
> And tightening up the strings,
> He played a melody, pure and sweet
> As sweet as the angel sings.
>
> The music ceased and the auctioneer
> With a voice that was quiet and low,
>
> Said "What now am I bid for this old violin?"
> As he held it aloft with its bow.

"One thousand, one thousand, Do I hear two?
"Two thousand, who makes it three?
"Three thousand once, three thousand twice,
"Going and gone," said he.

The audience cheered,
But some of them cried,
"We just don't understand.
"What changed its worth?"
Swift came the reply.
"The Touch of the Masters Hand."

And many a man with life out of tune
All battered and bruised with hardship
Is auctioned cheap to a thoughtless crowd
Much like that old violin

A mess of pottage, a glass of wine,
A game and he travels on.
He is going once, he is going twice,
He is going and almost gone.

But the Master comes,
And the foolish crowd never can quite understand,
The worth of a soul and the change that is wrought
By the Touch of the Master's Hand.

—Myra Brooks Welch[40]

Your Incredible Worth

Let me release another blessing over you, my beloved teen:

May the truth be forever etched in your heart that you were never made to be "auctioned cheap." Regardless of what you've experienced or how you've felt about yourself, I bless you with the touch of the Master's Hand in this moment and beyond. May you clearly see your incredible worth and forever leave the brokenness of the past behind. May your entire life be a melody, pure and sweet.

Making It Your Reality

In the remaining chapters you'll find many practical reset strategies designed to help you experience the reality of your incredible worth. I pray you'll not only read the strategies but also put them into practice.

Chapter 10 Reflections

Did you know?	Repentance before God means changing your mind—turning 180 degrees and going in the direction of God's path.
Words to Live By	But if we own up to our sins, God shows that He is faithful and just by forgiving us of our sins and purifying us from the pollution of all the bad things we have done. (1 John 1:9, The Voice) "If you have given your virginity away, it is not too late to start over. You cannot get your virginity back, but God can give you a fresh start." (Rose Publishing, *Why Wait?*)
From Your Heart	**Your affirmation:** I trust God's heart of mercy for me. I open my heart now to receive forgiveness and freedom from the burdens of guilt, pain, shame, or trauma. I fully embrace God's grace pathway that resets my sexuality and gives me a fresh start.

Chapter 11

You Have a Way of Escape

One of the many fascinating things about God is that He knows everything all at once and nothing takes Him by surprise. He is all-knowing, or omniscient. This means that your sexual struggles and unhealthy choices don't catch Him off guard. He planned your way of escape before you were even born.

Before God created Adam and Eve, He knew they would use their gift of free will to choose their own way instead of His. God gave them free will anyway because that's how true love works. True love doesn't force its way on anyone. Before they made the choice in Eden, God knew the outcome. And before they even became aware of the outcome, He provided the solution to cover their shame and reset their lives. Again, that's just how true love works—it always seeks what's best for you!

First Corinthians 10:13

First Corinthians 10:13 in The Passion Translation is our anchor verse for this chapter, and it's worth reading a few times:

We all experience times of testing, which is normal for every human being. But God will be faithful to you. He will screen and filter the severity, nature, and timing of every test or trial you face so that you can bear it. And each test is an opportunity to trust him more, for along with every trial God has provided for you ***a way of escape*** *that will bring you out of it victoriously* (emphasis mine).

God Has Many Customized Doors of Escape

God has a customized way of escape for every single sexual temptation you'll ever face. You also have a responsibility—first, to desire a way out of the temptation instead of indulging. Second, to take the necessary action to benefit from the way of escape God has provided. That means there are two sides to the way of escape out of sexual temptations: God's and yours. The two sides need to work together. Let's find out some of what's involved on each side.

Story Bite

There was a point in my young adult years when I felt the strong love of my Heavenly Father pulling me away from the path I was on. He was giving me a way of escape, but I had the nerve to tell Him, "Not now!" Of course, He didn't push. Once again, I missed it, but you don't have to. Be willing to take the way of escape God gives you!

—Auntie Marva

God's Provision

The complete victory of Jesus

While on earth, Jesus experienced every temptation known to humanity, yet He never sinned.[41] This means that He's able to relate to whatever you go through. It also means that when you enter a spiritual life-union with Jesus, His complete victory becomes your victory, and that changes everything! In this battle with sexual temptation, you're fighting FROM victory, not FOR victory.

God's own spiritual armour

God gives you His own powerful armour for your protection and to resist Satan's assaults. You'll need to wear every part as described in Ephesians 6:10–18:

Truth as a belt that strengthens and sets you free.

Righteousness that comes from Jesus as your body armour to keep your heart pure.

Peace as shoes for you to stand alert and ready.

Faith as a wrap-around shield to intercept every fiery arrow that Satan throws at you.

Salvation as a helmet to cover your head and ears so your thoughts are protected from lies.

God's Word spoken from your mouth as a sharp spiritual sword.

Prayer of all kinds that are fitting for different situations.

When you put on this armour, you're clothing yourself with the victorious presence of Jesus.[42]

The Spirit of grace

God gives you His Spirit of unmerited favour and power to work in you and do what you cannot do in your natural human strength. His supernatural power flows in and through you.

Words of wisdom

God's Words of Wisdom give you the ability to see the many snares that Satan uses. He often works through circumstances, people, and the culture. God has dedicated the entire book of Proverbs, with its thirty-one chapters, just to wisdom. These chapters cover every aspect of life, including sexual temptations. Reading a chapter each day and meditating on what you read will deposit in your heart the wisdom you need to make wise choices.

Jesus is wisdom wrapped up in a person.[43] When you pursue wisdom as a priority, you'll learn to see through the eyes of Jesus and think like Him. Eventually you'll come to experience the blessing of God in each area of your life.

Community God has given you supportive relationships within your family, church, and wider community. Like me, many have learned valuable lessons from difficult experiences. Why not learn from the experiences of others instead of repeating them? Although it may be awkward, having honest conversations with a parent or guardian about the struggles you're having is your Plan A. But if that doesn't work out, you have other options. Speak to a youth ministry pastor or the leader of a faith-based community program and ask them to connect you with a mentor or accountability partner.[44] Becoming accountable to someone with whom you can share honestly on a regular basis is a really wise move.

Your Responsibility

Be willing Be willing to take the way of escape God provides for you. And if you're not willing, ask God to give you a wise and courageous heart that's willing to take His side in the battle.

Tap into the victory of Jesus The blood of Jesus and the Name of Jesus are the spiritual access codes that enable you to tap into the victory that Jesus won on your behalf. Jesus defeated Satan at the cross and made it possible for you to overcome sexual temptations. Your victory also comes through the Spirit and Word of God.

- "And they have defeated him by the blood of the Lamb and by their testimony."[45]
- "Your strength and prowess will not be enough ... but My Spirit will be."[46]

The Name of Jesus represents all that Jesus is and all that He has done, and that's why praying in the Name of Jesus is so powerful. By saying "in the Name of Jesus" when you pray, you're doing so much more than mouthing a cliché or following a Christian routine. You're connecting with the person of Jesus, His victory, power, and authority. It's as if you're wrapping up your prayer and sending it off with supernatural force.

Dedicate your body to God Your parents may have dedicated you as a baby to the Lord. (Also called "baby christening"). Now as a teenager, it's your responsibility to willingly present your body to God. Today's culture treats the human body as if its main purpose is for sexual pleasure. There's so much pressure to use your body in ways that are not pleasing to God. You now know, however, that your body is designed for higher purposes. God promises to keep and guard whatever you willingly set apart for His purposes.

Refuse to copy the world Romans 12:1–2 makes a powerful appeal and provides you with guidance to overcome the pressures you'll face from the culture around you.

"I plead with you to give your bodies to God because of all he has done for you. Let them be a living and holy sacrifice—the kind he will find acceptable. This is truly the way to worship him. Don't copy the behavior and customs of this world, but let God transform you into a new person by changing the way you think. Then you will learn to know God's will for you, which is good and pleasing and perfect." (NLT)

Have a plan of action You need to develop a practical action plan in order to experience the benefits of God's plan of escape.

The next chapter gives you the framework for a plan that puts the experience of sexual wholeness within your reach.

Chapter 11 Reflections

Did you know?

You're never alone in your sexual struggles and temptations because God is with you to help you.

Words to Live By

"The problem is, when we're faced with temptation, we aren't looking for the escape. Maybe we enjoy our secret sin too much, and we don't truly want God's help." (Mary Fairchild)

Don't you know that flirting with the world's values places you at odds with God? Whoever chooses to be the world's friend makes himself God's enemy. (James 4:4b, TPT)

From Your Heart

Your affirmation: I have courage and strength from God to responsibly take the way of escape out of sexual temptations. My heart willingly chooses and follows the pathway of God's wisdom. I put my faith in the blood and in the Name of Jesus to help me overcome.

Chapter 12

Five Practical Ps for Sexual Wholeness

Benjamin Franklin, a former president of the United States, once said, "*If you fail to plan, you are planning to fail!*" He may not have had your sexuality in mind, but his words of wisdom certainly apply to you experiencing sexual wholeness. God has provided you with a way of escape for the sexual struggles you'll go through, and we're ready to develop a plan to put it into action.

Story Bite

After many sexual struggles, I took a youth discipleship class. The program was like a lifeline that changed the direction of my life. Being trained in principles from the Bible prepared me to honour my body and make healthy sexual choices. I'm so grateful that I had mentors who battled in prayer for my sexuality.

—Sophia

We'll be using five "P" words to build the framework of your practical escape plan. Sexual wholeness will be well within your reach as you diligently put the plan into action.

1. Prioritize
2. Plan
3. Prepare
4. Picture
5. Persevere

Prioritize

Set your mind to give first place to honouring God's intent for sex, not your personal pleasure. When you pursue God's wisdom and purpose first, then all other things will be added to you.[47]

- Put Jesus first, no matter what, for He is your main escape door for fleeing sexual temptations. He is your first resort, not last. Talk to Him honestly about your weaknesses and call on Him during your struggles. When the Bible says we're to pray with all kinds of prayers and on every occasion, it includes praying about sexual matters.
- Practise a consciousness of the presence of Jesus with you, even when your thoughts may not be pure or you're engaging in activities that may not be pleasing to Him.
- Fix your eyes on Jesus and see His eyes blazing with love for you. He promised to keep in perfect peace (wholeness) the one whose mind is fixed on Him.
- Do not leave God out of the picture or try to put your sexuality in an "off limits" zone. Remember that it isn't possible to separate your sexuality from your spirituality.

Plan

Use the fire drills you've done in school as a model or template to develop your own "sexual fire drill."

- Know where your exits are.
- Know the fire escape route.
- Know who to call for help before the fire gets out of hand. This isn't the time to call a friend who you know is also struggling with sexual issues. Jesus says, "Come to me first!" He does want you to have a community to draw on, but invites you to call on Him first. Push back embarrassment. Call on Jesus and reach out to others who will help you follow the path of God's truth instead of your feelings.
- Avoid the elevator. There may be times when the sexual passion in your body will feel like fire. The temptation will be to find the quickest "fix." It's like taking the elevator when there's a real fire. Don't do it! You may get stuck. Or even worse, the elevator shaft may break and you end up plummeting to the bottom. Think back to the chapter on "False Starts Are Costly" and you'll see what I mean.

Put your escape plan in writing. It's a work in progress, so you'll need to revisit and revise it as often as necessary. What should be included? The many secrets you've been learning about God's design for sex and your sexuality will guide you. Your plan needs to align with God's plan. Here are a few tips:

- Write in your own words what you now understand about sex, your sexuality, and the urges you feel in your body. For example, "Sex isn't a pastime. My sexuality is a precious gift from God, and I will treasure it. I will not mistake sex for love."
- Be honest with yourself about any triggers that push you into temptation, such as when you're feeling tired, lonely, depressed,

rejected, stressed, or bored. Include some ideas on how you can avoid being trapped by these feelings.

- Guard against association with peers who could influence you to get on the wrong path.[48]
- Decide ahead of time what you will and will not do. This has to do with boundaries, which we'll go into a bit more in the next chapter.
- Write down the names and contact information for persons in your support community to whom you will be accountable. If you do not have mentors or accountability partners, ask God to help you establish those relationships.
- Write down scriptures that you'll memorize and meditate on to strengthen your mind against temptations. You'll need them before, during, and after.

Prepare

Preparation includes practice. Even professional athletes practise their skills. By the time Olympic sprinters get into the starting blocks for a race, they would have spent years preparing their mind and body. They would have practised the starting commands and routines thousands of times to avoid a false start.

- Invite persons from your support community, such as a mentor or your youth pastor, to be part of your preparation. Allow them to fill the role that coaches do in an athlete's development. Share your plan with them or seek their assistance in developing one.
- Daily put on the spiritual armour that God has provided for you.
- Daily train your mind with what I call *Power8Thinking*™ from Philippians 4:8—Occupying your mind with whatever is true, noble, right, pure, lovely, admirable, excellent, and praiseworthy.

- Daily re-dedicate your body for God's purposes.
- Fast the "junk food" from social media and other sources that weakens your spiritual immune system.
- Feast on the Word of God and other sources of wisdom.

Picture

Your imagination is a powerful gift from God. Where your sexuality is concerned, God wants you to use it to picture yourself living a life of sexual wholeness, united in a bond of endless love with Him.

Satan's plan, on the other hand, is to hijack your imagination and use it for his purposes—to picture yourself indulging in sexual workarounds instead of escaping the temptations. Should Satan succeed in hijacking your imagination, you can quickly take it back by rebooting your mind with practical techniques such as these:

- Change the scenery (your physical location).
- Do something different.
- Take a cold shower.

- Go for a jog.
- Hold an ice cube in your hand.
- Change the kind of images you're looking at. In the words of the Bible, "turn your eyes from looking at worthless things."[49] This means you are to guard your "eye gate."
- Play the kind of music that will move your heart closer to God. That's guarding your "ear gate."
- Speak audibly what God says about you and your sexuality. Words are powerful, especially words from the Bible. Everything in the universe, including your body, was created by God's Word and responds to His Word. Angels respond to God's Word as well, and they'll come to your aid when they hear you giving voice to God's Word.[50]
- Read aloud from the "Reboot Your Mind Collection" in the Bonus Section at the end of the book. This tool pulls together in one place for easy access all of the "Words to Live By" from each chapter and a few extras.
- Pray! A good prayer in these moments is to ask your Heavenly Father to cleanse the hallways of your imagination with the blood of Jesus. The Bible says He is faithful and will do precisely that.[51]

From what you read earlier about the Marshmallow Test; you'll recall how some of the children used their imagination to help them wait. You have the same gift of imagination and can also use it to help you wait in the *Not Yet!* zone.

Persevere

Keep getting back up again, regardless of how many times you may fall for temptation. As the Bible says, *"The godly may trip seven times, but they will get up again."*[52]

Never fall for Satan's trick of secrecy. He'll get you to try and hide what has happened from your support community. He'll even want you to repeat Adam and Eve's mistake of trying to hide from God. But you do need support to get back up again. Seek the help of your support community to help you rework stronger boundaries into your action plan.

Above all, overcome thoughts of condemnation and shame by running into the loving embrace of your Heavenly Father. Going to God and acknowledging your need for forgiveness and cleansing is a sign of humility. That's a good thing to do, for God promises to give more grace to the humble. [53] Prayer is your number one perseverance strategy!

Remember that should you have a false start; it doesn't change your Heavenly Father's love for you. Because His love is perfect, He can never love you any less or any more than He already does. You're going to read more about that in the last chapter.

Chapter 12 Reflections

Did you know?	You've basically planned to fail if you try going through your teen years without an action plan for overcoming sexual temptation.
Words to Live By	"Surround yourself with only people who are going to lift you higher." (Oprah Winfrey) "Sometimes when we think we are strong enough we don't take the necessary steps to protect ourselves from falling into temptation." (Pam Stenzel)
From Your Heart	**Your Prayer:** I thank you, Heavenly Father, that you still love me even when I fall for temptation and make the wrong choice. I'm grateful that because of your great love for me, I can get back up again. Amen.

Chapter 13

Protect What You Love

Your practical escape action plan includes setting boundaries. It's such a major part of the plan that I've dedicated a whole chapter to boundaries. We've all inherited a natural dislike for boundaries from Adam and Eve. It's obvious even in a two-year-old. Still, it doesn't change the fact that boundaries serve an important purpose in our lives—they protect what we love.

Think of a personal possession you really treasure. It may be something you paid a lot of money for or waited a long time to get. If you have siblings, you protect it from them with an actual or imaginary "off limits" sign. You may also reserve it for special occasions, like a pair of expensive Nikes that you wear only when there's no rain or snow in the forecast because you don't want them to get dirty. You know what it means to have boundaries for material things like shoes, clothes, jewellery, even special snacks. The question is, doesn't your body also deserve boundaries? As you now know, God places extremely high value on your sexuality. Do you?

What God Had in Mind

Having read this far, you realize that my approach to the sexual aspect of your teenage journey is to help you discover and honour the *Big Ideas* God had in mind when He invented sex. God loves every cell of your body and considers your body sacred. You now know that God designed sex for marriage between a man and a woman and gave it greater spiritual meaning. Sex and marriage are icons pointing to the divine exchange of endless love you and I are created to share with God. It only makes sense for something so sacred to have high-level security and protection!

I've had young people and adults ask me whether the fruit that Adam and Eve ate in the Garden of Eden was sex. I don't know. But this is what I do know. When God told them not to eat from the Tree of Knowledge, it was for their own good. He put the boundary in place to protect them, but Satan (the serpent) lied and said that God was holding back on them. They fell for the lie.

Prerequisites for Healthy Sexual Boundaries

A New Mindset

In order to set and keep healthy sexual boundaries, you'll need a new mindset about God's intentions. God isn't a party pooper, killjoy, or "wowser." He's not old fashioned, and He's not trying to make life difficult for you. God placed the marriage boundary around sex as a gift to protect you from pain.

Word Gem

A person without self-control is like a city with broken down walls.

Proverbs 25:28

A Strong Why

If you don't have a strong reason for sexual boundaries, you may set them, but you won't keep them. Or you may not set any at all. A strong reason for sexual boundaries is to honour God, yourself, and the other person in your relationship.

Dating doesn't have to equal sex if you set relationship boundaries and stick to them. You're setting yourself up for failure if the standards you use to set your boundaries are based on actions, such as these commonly asked questions: How far is too far? How far can we go? Is it okay to do this or that?

Some Tips for Setting Sexual Boundaries

Setting sexual boundaries honours your part of the responsibility for the Way of Escape action plan.

- Write out your plan to increase your commitment to it.
- Recognize that creating sexual boundaries is a process and not a one-time exercise. As you discover more about yourself and the other person, you'll need to make changes. More than likely, you'll need to tighten up, not lighten up, on the boundaries.
- Acknowledge your unique weaknesses and strengths. There's no one-size-fits-all template. Cuddling, for example, may trigger temptations in one person but not in another.
- Customize your sexual boundaries. God has a customized way of escape for each temptation you encounter. You also need to customize your escape plan. Remember to include personal boundaries to protect your thoughts.

- Be honest with yourself. Be self-aware and take time to honestly evaluate the temptations you've had and the things that are likely to trip you up.
- Ask the Holy Spirit for guidance. He knows you better than you know yourself.
- Set your boundaries early because timing is everything. The advantage of establishing sexual boundaries before you start a relationship is that you can make the other person aware of them right away. If they resist the idea of boundaries, it's a red flag that this relationship isn't for you.
- Be strong in your conviction when sharing your boundaries. The other person will be able to detect how committed you are.
- Stick to your boundaries. Don't be wishy-washy like the boy in the Marshmallow Test. You'll recall that he right away set the boundary that they weren't going to eat the marshmallow. But almost instantly he turned to the girl, wondering what they were going to do.

Avoid These Set-ups

There are certain actions and behaviours to avoid if you sincerely want to live by the sexual boundaries you create. Here are some ideas that will protect you from setting yourself up to break those boundaries:

- Limit the time you spend alone with the other person.
- Dress appropriately. Your clothing can be a major source of temptation for yourself and others.
- Keep your clothes on.
- Stay out of bed with the other person.
- Limit physical contact (touching, hugging, kissing).

- Spend time getting to know more about each other by talking about topics such as education, faith beliefs, career plans, hobbies, family, and friends.
- Choose temptation-free environments. Whether it's the place you hang out or the atmosphere you create when you're together, it's always wise to avoid "hot spots."
- Stay away from drinking alcohol and using drugs, as they numb your senses.

The Difference a Name Makes

A few years ago, I had the privilege of doing a birthday blessing ceremony for a young adult by the name of Sabrina. As I usually do, I used my special resource book to find the inherent meaning and the spiritual significance of her name, as well as the associated scripture.

Meanings of Sabrina: Boundary Line and Protected.

Life Verse: The boundary lines have fallen for me in pleasant places. (Psalm 16:6, NIV)

During the ceremony, I spoke a blessing over her life based on the meanings of her name and her life verse. Her discovery that both her name and life verse had to do with boundary lines changed everything for her. She realized that having sexual and other boundaries in her life honoured God, herself, and others. Some time later, she wrote: "The experience launched me on a brand new, less destructive trajectory."

Reinforcing Your Sexual Wholeness Commitment

Writing out your sexual escape plan is physical evidence of your sexual wholeness commitment to God, yourself, and the person you'll marry someday. You can reinforce your commitment with the following Pledge of Sexual Honour. I encourage you to speak the Pledge often because your words do release spiritual molecules to create your desired reality.

Ready. Set. Not Yet!
Pledge of Sexual Honour

I understand that God designed sex for marriage as a bond of intimacy that physically, emotionally, and physically unites a man and woman in a covenant relationship.

I am committed to honouring God's design for sex and marriage, although the culture around me has its own views and opinions about sex.

I am committed to waiting until I am joined with my husband or wife in marriage to engage in sexual activity. I will honour my future husband or wife by saving sex for marriage as God intended.

I am committed to honouring my body and keeping it free from all forms of sexual workarounds in order to fulfill God's intention for my body as a holy and majestic place for His Spirit to dwell in.

I am committed to receiving forgiveness and cleansing through the blood of Jesus for all past or future sexual experiences that violate my pledge of sexual honour.

I make this pledge today believing that the power of God's grace will preserve and keep me in sexual wholeness.

Chapter 13 Reflections

Did you know?

God loves every part of your body, and He places extremely high value on your sexuality.

Words to Live By

"When the purpose of a thing is not known, abuse is inevitable." (Dr. Myles Munroe)

There is a sense in which sexual sins are different from all others. In sexual sin we violate the sacredness of our own bodies, these bodies that were made for God-given and God-modeled love, for "becoming one" with another. (1 Corinthians 6:18, The Message)

From Your Heart

Your Affirmation: I will resist the pressure to date just because of what others are doing. I'm anchored in the perfect love of my Heavenly Father and will not go looking for love in the wrong places. I diligently stick to boundaries that honour God, myself, and others.

____

____

____

____

____

____

____

Chapter 14

See Your Future Now

There's something more you'll need on this journey into sexual wholeness—Vision. I don't mean natural eyesight. By vision, I mean seeing from your heart a clear mental picture of your desired future—your destination. (Remember that your spiritual heart is the source of your imagination and thoughts). This mental picture will daily motivate you to put your Way of Escape action plan into practice, stick to your boundaries, and live up to your Pledge of Sexual Honour.

Vision enlarges on the fourth "P" (Picture) in the framework of your action plan. This involves using the gift of imagination God gave you to picture what sexual wholeness would look like for you. Vision will empower you to resist temptations. It will inspire you to live according to God's design for sex and your sexuality. It will inspire you to save sex for marriage as God intended.

The Champion Athlete

So far, sprinters in the starting blocks waiting for the official start of a race have been good examples to learn from about timing, waiting, and false starts. Let's see what we can learn from them about vision.

You'll recall from Chapter 2 that a big part of their preparation is the development of a mental picture of their desired future. In the words of author Dr. Stephen R. Covey, we can say that they "begin with the end in mind." Here's what that means: *"Begin With the End in Mind is based on imagination—the ability to envision in your mind what you cannot at present see with your eyes. It is based on the principle that all things are created twice.*"[54] Likewise, in this *Not Yet!* zone of your teenage journey, developing a mental picture of your desired goal of sexual wholeness is a high priority for you. You'll need to first envision yourself there then take the necessary practical steps to make it your reality.

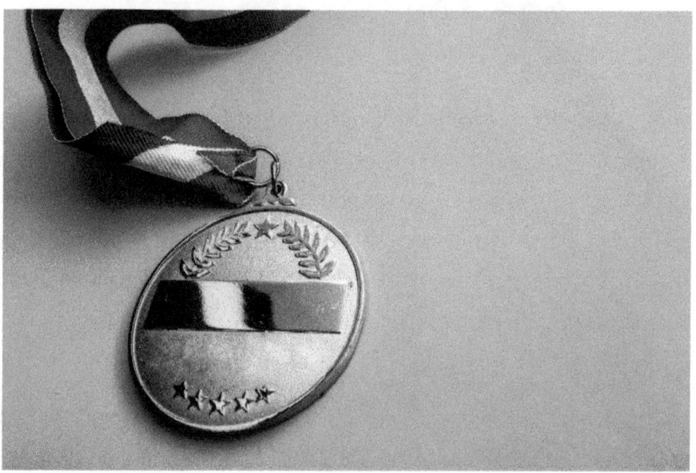

By identifying some of what vision does for champion athletes, you'll get a really good idea of how seeing your future now will also benefit you. Here are a few examples of what vision does for athletes:

- Gives them goals with which to align their choices.
- Enables them to identify and resist distractions.
- Gives them perseverance to turn challenges into opportunities for growth.
- Motivates them to play by the rules to avoid disqualification.
- Makes them willing to live with constraints or restrictions that will help them in the long run to be a better competitor.

- Inspires them to guard the health and overall wellbeing of their bodies, even to the point of avoiding "junk food."
- Keeps their minds focused.
- Cultivates the discipline to endure strict, regimented training and preparation routines.
- Empowers them to endure short-term pain for long-term gain.

"Sacrificial living" is a good way to describe the lifestyle of a champion athlete. Their commitment to making the mental picture they have of their future become a reality is the fuel for their sacrificial lifestyle.

How about you? Do you have a clear enough mental picture of the desired future for your sexuality and for your life as a whole? What does this "destination" look like?

The Problem with No Destination

"If you don't know where you are going, any road will get you there." This brilliant statement sums up a conversation between Alice and the Cheshire Cat in the book *Alice in Wonderland*. As I think about the need for you to have a clear picture of your desired future, I imagine us having the same conversation, me as the Cheshire Cat and you as Alice (or Allan if you're a male).

"Would you tell me, please, which way I ought to go from here?"

"That depends a good deal on where you want to get to," said the Cat.

"I don't much care where—" said Alice (Allan).

"Then it doesn't matter which way you go," said the Cat.

"—so long as I get somewhere," Alice (Allan) added as an explanation.

"Oh, you're sure to do that," said the Cat, "if you only walk long enough."

Where You Ought to Go from Here

Vision is a bridge that connects you to your future. The whole purpose of *Ready. Set. Not Yet!* is to help you discover "where you ought to go from here" and to help you map out your way to get there. I trust you've figured out by now that God has already designed the destination for your sexuality. As a recap, God designed sex for marriage between a man and a woman. He also designed marriage to represent the exchange of endless love that you and I are created to share with God.

With this destination plugged into your "spiritual GPS," you'll have the privilege of arriving in God's best timing. You'll avoid delays caused by accidents. You'll have the best route mapped out for you. Above all, you'll avoid speed traps and costly speeding tickets.

The Bible captures the importance of vision in this proverb: "Where there is no vision, the people perish."[55] The Hebrew word used here for perish is *paw-rah'* with the associated imagery of a woman's hair flowing unrestrained in the wind, directionless and blown in all directions.[56] By the way, this imagery applies whether you're male or female.

Destination does matter! You're not just trying to get "somewhere." You're destined for the greatness God had in mind when He created you. It's not just any road that's going to get you there.

Getting You There

Now let's look at some essentials for mapping out your vision route.

Prerequisites You'll need to answer these two questions from God's perspective: Who am I? Why am I here? Another person's perspective, even yours, may be distorted.

Who Am I? You're God's beloved, an original masterpiece, chosen! You belong to the King of the universe, who is your Heavenly Father. That makes you royalty, not someone for whom anything goes.

Prerequisites (cont'd)

God shared His Spirit essence with you, made you with a soul, and formed a male or female body for you. He designed you this way for you to share a divine exchange of endless love. The ultimate purpose of your body is to become the holy place (majestic habitation) in which the Spirit of God lives. That's why it matters how you use your body.

Why Am I Here? You're here on the earth at this time because God sent you here on purpose. You're His solution to a problem that existed before you were born. You're destined to make a unique contribution to the world and the kingdom of God. There's greatness in you!

Awareness of generational matters

Your vision must be bigger than yourself. In this way, your motivation for sexual wholeness will be bigger than the urges in your body and the temptations you face.

You're a link to past and future generations.

The choices of yesterday's generations have helped to shape you, and your choices will help shape tomorrow's generations.

When it comes to sexual matters, your choices are creating a legacy for the next generation. Your choices carry a responsibility, not only for yourself but for future generations also. So live the future now that you desire for future generations (including the children you'll have in God's appointed time). You can't afford to be short-sighted. You have the privilege of being more aware than previous generations. Use your privilege wisely.

Faith, courage, character, and grace

To get to your destination of sexual wholeness, you'll need to travel on these roads called faith, courage, character, and grace. They're not automatic. You must be intentional about cultivating these pathways.

Vison is seeing by faith. Bringing your future into the present will require you having faith in God and in yourself. Your faith in God will only be as strong as the beliefs you have about Him. Believing that His love for you seeks only your best is top priority. Satan's number one temptation strategy is to lie about God's motives. He succeeded with Adam and Eve but failed with Jesus. Let his attempts with you fail also! Faith in yourself will help you to build character and move steadily forward in experiencing God's design for your sexuality.

It requires courage to take the "road less travelled" and to stick with unpopular values, morals, and truths.

You'll need to build the character qualities of commitment, discipline, self-control, and perseverance in the same way that an athlete trains and prepares to become a champion.

Grace, as you know, is the provision God made for you to start over, knowing that you may mess up along the way.

Make the Vision Plain

"Write the vision and make it plain upon tablets."[57]

That was God's instruction to an Old Testament prophet named Habakkuk. He is giving you the same instruction.

God gave Habakkuk a further explanation:

> *Write it out in big block letters so that it can be read on the run. This vision-message is a witness pointing to what's coming. It aches for the coming—it can hardly wait! And it doesn't lie. If it seems slow in coming, wait. It's on its way. It will come right on time.*[58]

There are some significant points in this explanation you don't want to miss. They're extremely relevant for creating the mental picture of your sexual wholeness destination. Here they are:

- It can be read on the run (while fleeing temptation).
- It's pointing to what's coming (you don't have it yet, but you hope for it because you see it through eyes of faith).
- It aches for the coming—it can hardly wait! (Sounds familiar, doesn't it?)
- It doesn't lie (The plans that God has for your sexuality are true, although they clash with the cultural views and opinions).
- It seems slow in coming, wait. (Timing is everything!)
- It's on its way. (Don't let doubt cause you to sabotage God's timing for your life).
- It will come right on time. (All things considered, God does have the best route mapped out to get you to your destination in the fastest possible time. He does make everything beautiful in its time).[59]

Fun Fact

Since writing tablets existed in Bible times, the iPad and other tablets aren't brand-new inventions. They're really technologically advanced models.

Your Sexuality Vision Board

I wish I'd done a sexuality vision board when I was your age. I missed it, but you don't have to! I recommend this practical and very powerful exercise for implementing God's instruction.

Like your Way of Escape action plan and your boundaries Pledge of Sexual Honour, write out your vision as an act of commitment. Of course, also include pictures, drawings, and words—whatever works for you and reflects God's design. With a vision board, you're doing for your mental picture of sexual wholeness what Google Maps does in mapping directions to a physical destination.

What will you include? Here are some suggestions:

- Photos of wedding ceremonies.
- Photos of married couples with their children.
- Qualities you desire in your spouse.
- Qualities and values you desire your children to have.
- The quality of relationship you desire to have with God.
- Images and words to motivate you toward sexual wholeness.
- Your academic and career goals.

- Images of what the fulfillment of your life's purpose would look like.

You may not get very far in your pursuit of sexual wholeness by trying to observe a set of rules, or even by repressing your feelings. I do believe, however, that by mentally bringing your future into the present, you'll be more conscious of what's at stake. You'll be more strongly motivated to redirect your passion and choose long-term gains over short-term pleasures.

Everything by Prayer

"*Prayer is not everything, but everything is by prayer.*" This quote from Armin Gesswin is based on Philippians 4:6. It's therefore fitting for me to end this chapter by releasing the prayer of Ephesians 1:18–19 from The Passion Translation on your behalf:

I pray that the light of God will illuminate the eyes of your imagination, flooding you with light, until you experience the full revelation of the hope of his calling—that is, the wealth of God's glorious inheritances that he finds in us, his holy ones!

I pray that you will continually experience the immeasurable greatness of God's power made available to you through faith. Then your lives will be an advertisement of this immense power as it works through you!

Amen!

Chapter 14 Reflections

Did you know?

The temporary pleasure of sexual workarounds can't be compared with the bright future and eternal rewards God has prepared for you.

Words to Live By

"You must get an image of what you want to be on the inside first if you want to see it come to pass in your life on the outside." (Joel Osteen)

"You make sexual choices not based on how you are feeling but by who you have chosen to become." (Julie Slattery)

From Your Heart

Your Prayer: Heavenly Father, I need your help to see my future more clearly. I ask for your inspiration and the inner strength to be courageous and fully committed as I go forward. Let your Word be a lamp to my feet and a light to my path. I pray these things in the Name of Jesus. Amen.

Chapter 15

Never Forget This One Thing

Congratulations! You're on the last chapter, and it's time for the ultimate *Ready. Set. Not Yet!* secret. Although this secret was like a thread weaved through each chapter, more visible in some than others, you now get to see it in full view.

Your success in honouring God's design for sex, your body, and those you're attracted to hinges on this one thing. When this truth is firmly rooted and grounded in your heart (the core of who you are), you'll be motivated from within to save sex for marriage, no matter what. You'll have built-in stamina and courage to resist the world's "anything goes" opinions about sex. You'll have inner strength to resist the temptation to engage in sexual workarounds for instant gratification. You'll have the inspiration you need to choose long-term gains over short-lived pleasures.

What's this one thing? It's this essential truth: **God has chosen you in love for Himself.** Let's unpack the seven words in that statement:

GOD	God is your beginning and Source. He is your Creator and Heavenly Father.
HAS	Past tense ... It's a done deal!

CHOSEN You've already been chosen by God, and He won't "unchoose" you. You're not an accident or mistake. You were hand-picked by God. Don't live as if you haven't been chosen.

YOU You're an original masterpiece. God knows every intimate detail about you. He knows your thoughts before you think them, even the number of hairs on your head.

IN You began in God. He conceived you in the womb of His mind long before your mother conceived you. You exist to be in God, and for God to be in you.

LOVE God created you in love, by love, and to love. You're God's beloved. You don't have to earn God's love. God loves all of you! He knows your imperfections, still He loves you perfectly. His love for you is unconditional and endless. Your Heavenly Father loves you with the same passionate love He has for Jesus. Love always seeks expression, which means you're loved to love. You love God because He first loved you. You love yourself because God loves you, and you love others as yourself.

FOR There's purpose behind your existence—a unique purpose that God determined before you were conceived. You represent and express attributes of God that no one else does.

HIMSELF You belong! Your ultimate destination is life-union with God in an exchange of endless love forever.

The Ultimate Secret

Knowing and believing that God has chosen you in love for Himself will fill up whatever is missing in your motivation to pursue sexual wholeness.

Based on Einstein's perspective, this one thing is the ultimate secret or *Big Idea* from the mind of God that explains the designs He built into sex and the human body. As Einstein said, "The rest are details." This one *Big Idea* explains why God created you a male or a female and why He designed sex for marriage. It also explains the advance rescue plan that God designed to reset all of humanity after we abused our gift of free will.

The ultimate expression of God's love for you is paying in full with His own sacred blood for all your violations that separate you from Him (your sins). Yes, His *own* blood! It's generally understood that the blood of Jesus paid for all of humanity's sin. But what's not often recognized is that it was actually the holy blood of God the Father that flowed from the body of Jesus at His crucifixion. From the scriptures we understand that the Heavenly Father prepared the human body for baby Jesus and carried out His conception in Mary's womb through the work of the Holy Spirit. [60] The angel therefore announced to Mary that "the baby to be born will be holy."[61] You see, God had to pay with His own blood because sacred blood was the only perfect payment for humanity's sin. The virgin birth of Jesus is really an expression of God's love, guaranteeing the purity of the blood of Jesus as the perfect payment to restore fallen humanity, including you and me, back to Himself.

Beloved is Who You Really Are

You truly are centre stage in God's great love story! This truth that God chose you in love for Himself is your greatest identity definition. Seeing yourself as purposefully chosen and loved changes everything. Satan will do his very best to steal this truth from your heart as he did with Adam and Eve in Eden. Thankfully, he failed when he tried with Jesus. Because Jesus won, you can win too.

Don't Let Satan Leave It Out

As soon as Jesus came out of the water at His baptism in the River Jordan, He received the affirmation of His Heavenly Father: "This is my Beloved Son with whom I am well pleased."[62]

Jesus then entered a period of fasting for forty days in the wilderness, and at the end Satan took advantage of His extreme hunger. Satan proposed the solution of turning stones into bread. But he prefaced the proposal with a distorted echo of the identity affirmation Jesus had received from the Father. Satan said: "If you are the Son of God, tell these stones to become bread."[63] Satan repeated the same distorted echo in his second temptation. This time it was to get Jesus to jump off the top of the temple building. Both temptations were attempts for Jesus to use His power in ways that were not authorized by the Father.

Did you notice the difference between the Father's affirmation and Satan's echo? The Father had said, "This is my *Beloved* Son ..." Satan said, "If you are the Son of God ..." What's the difference? Satan left out the main thing. He always does! The Father had affirmed Jesus, not only as His Son, but as His BELOVED Son.

Be on guard. Satan is using the same strategy to take advantage of your longings (hunger) for intimacy. He invades your mind with thoughts to overshadow the truth that you're God's beloved and that your Heavenly Father in His goodness will meet all your needs. Once Satan succeeds in dislodging the truth from your heart that you are God's beloved, he intensifies your "hunger" and rushes you off to look for love. When you're disconnected from the truth that you're God's beloved, you end up looking for love in the wrong places and settling for counterfeits. Settling for counterfeits is like trying to fit a square peg into a round hole. Sexual workarounds do not answer your deep inner need for love and intimacy. It's a compromise!

Plug In

My desire for you is that sooner than later you'll plug into your Heavenly Father's endless love for you and allow His love to satisfy the longings of your heart. As you know, when an object is plugged into an electrical source, it receives a power flow from that source. In the same way, when you remain plugged into the power of your Heavenly Father's love for you, you begin to see yourself through His eyes of love. The power of His great love in your heart also becomes an invincible force against sexual temptations.

This Thing Called Love

You are made for the Godkind of love. Other forms of love (family, friendship, marital love) all have their place, but it's in this Godkind of love that you'll find ultimate satisfaction. A huge challenge that you'll need to overcome in your pursuit of sexual wholeness is the tendency to mistake physical, sexual attraction for true love.

First Corinthians 13 is the love chapter of the Bible. It defines true love by the following qualities:

- Patient.
- Kind (gentle and consistently kind).
- Not jealous, boastful, proud, or rude.
- Does not demand its own way.
- Not irritable.
- Keeps no record of wrongs.
- Does not rejoice in injustice.
- Rejoices when the truth wins out.
- Never gives up.
- Never loses faith.
- Is always hopeful.
- Endures through every circumstance.
- Lasts forever.

The *Ready. Set. Not Yet!* Edition

Let me condense these qualities into a *Ready. Set. Not Yet!* yardstick. You can use the following list to evaluate whether the feelings you have for someone, or the feelings they have for you, are really love.

- Waits on God's timing.
- Never hasty to make out or have sex.
- Believes the truth of God's design for sex.
- Seeks what's best from God's perspective.
- Sacrifices short-term pleasures for long-term gain.
- Believes that God has good things in store.
- Respects your sexual boundaries and has boundaries of their own.

- Gets back up again and resets after a slip.

My Story

I first had a glimpse of my Heavenly Father's love for me at the age of fourteen during a Good Friday church service. Deep in my heart I became aware that the crucifixion of Jesus was a huge demonstration of God's love for me *personally*. That day I opened my heart to Jesus and received Him as my Saviour. However, later on I struggled in my faith and eventually became tired of wearing myself out trying to love God.

I was well into my adult years when I discovered that I had the wrong focus. Instead of focusing on trying to love God, I needed to focus on how much God loved me. I started to shift my focus using Romans 5:5, which says that the love of God is poured out into my heart by the Holy Spirit. I started asking the Holy Spirit to pour the love of the Father into my heart. Little by little my heart became captivated by the Heavenly Father's love for me. What had been such a struggle in the earlier years eventually became almost effortless. I soon found my heart beating on its own with sincere love for my Heavenly Father—the love deposited there by the Holy Spirit.

The overflow of this love from my heart brought results far beyond anything I could have imagined. Many of the temptations I'd once battled gradually faded. Love had won! My love relationship with the Father won over my love for everything else. By the way, this isn't an age thing. Falling in love with the Heavenly Father is very much possible at your age and stage of life.

Your Story

So how will being plugged into your Heavenly Father's love for you impact your story? Having your conscious thoughts dominated by the truth that God has chosen you in love for Himself prepares you mentally and physically to sacrifice self gratification for love's sake. When this truth is settled in your heart, love will begin to override your desire to please yourself. Your greatest motivation for honouring God's design for sex is a conscious awareness of how much He loves you, not how much you love Him.

Your Generational Legacy

You have a generational purpose. Therefore, living with a consciousness of your Heavenly Father's love for you will not only change everything for you. It's also the one thing that could change everything for the generation you'll eventually parent. The Father's love that you're seeking to plug into now will be quite organic or "natural" for them. I see this firsthand with one of my goddaughters and her siblings. Their parents have nurtured their identity as God's beloved from the womb. It's organic to them—like a first spiritual language they won't forget.

I think of how comfortable three, four, and five-year-old children are with a cell phone and an iPad. Technology is native to them because they're born and raised in a technology-saturated environment, especially those whose parents are techies. This same principle applies to the Heavenly Father's love. The Father's love is "native" to children that are conceived, nurtured in the womb, born and raised in an atmosphere and environment that's saturated with Father's love.

It's not too early for you to have a mental picture of parenting such a generation—at God's appointed time and in God's appointed way. Each child that's conceived deserves to be wanted and loved. Your pursuit of sexual wholeness guards against conceiving an unwanted child.

Kudos ... Applause!

You made it to the end! I'm so proud of you ... well done!

There's no complicated action plan to create for this top secret. It's quite simple:

- Concentrate on what the Bible says about God's love for you.
- Ask the Holy Spirit to awaken your heart to the truth of the Father's love so it becomes clear and real to you.
- Grow your consciousness of Father's love for you by getting to know Jesus more each day. Jesus is the Word made flesh. He is also the physical manifestation of the Father. As Jesus told one of His disciples, "Anyone who has seen me has seen the Father!"[64]
- Remember that as you focus on God's love for you, your love for Him will follow—almost effortlessly.

Finally, please share this ultimate message of *Ready. Set. Not Yet!* with others in your circle: **God has chosen you in love for Himself. When you embrace this truth, you're less likely to look for love in the wrong places or settle for counterfeits.**

Chapter 15 Reflections

Did you know?	The truth that God chose you in love for Himself is your greatest identity definition.
Words to Live By	So above all else, let love be the beautiful prize for which you run. (1 Corinthians 13:13b, TPT) For it is Christ's love that fuels our passion and motivates us, because we are absolutely convinced that he has given his life for all of us. (2 Corinthians 5:14, TPT)
From Your Heart	**Your Affirmation:** My heart is being awakened to believe and receive the perfect love that my Heavenly Father has or me. I highly value the privilege I have to experience and pass on this legacy of Father's love to the generations after me.

Section 3 Take-Aways

The Main Thing

Read these key points from the section and circle a number from 1–5 to indicate how much you have embraced each truth. *("1" is "I totally disagree" and "5" is "I agree completely.")*

Highlight the key points with a score of 3 or less and make them the focus of your prayer practice below.

A huge challenge I'll need to overcome in my pursuit of sexual wholeness is the tendency to mistake physical sexual attraction for true love. True love doesn't force its way on me, and it always seeks what's best for me.

1 2 3 4 5

I need a practical plan of action in order to get the most benefit from the customized way of escape God has prepared for me to overcome sexual temptation.

1 2 3 4 5

In case Satan hijacks my imagination, I can quickly take it back by rebooting my mind.

1 2 3 4 5

Should I fall for a temptation, I'll get back up again and run into the loving embrace of my Heavenly Father.

1 2 3 4 5

The Main Thing (cont'd.)

There's an open invitation from the Father for me to come and trade in my past for the new beginning Jesus purchased with His precious blood. Adam and Eve made the mistake of trying to hide from God, but I won't.

1 2 3 4 5

Dating doesn't have to involve sex if I set relationship boundaries and stick to them. I'll likely need to tighten up, not lighten up, on my sexual boundaries while dating.

1 2 3 4 5

I'm destined for the greatness that God had in mind when He create me. It's not just any road that's going to get me there.

1 2 3 4 5

God has chosen me in love for Himself. I won't look for love in the wrong places or settle for counterfeits.

1 2 3 4 5

Prayer Practice

Speak to your Heavenly Father and ask Him to help you with the key points above that you need to internalize more fully. You may wish to write your prayer, and remember to include anyone who may be having similar challenges.

Your Call to Action

Identify at least one action you're committed to taking based on something you discovered in this section. Remember to use your "memory tools."

____

____

____

____

____

____

____

A Blessing

Beloved teen, I bless you with an unforgettable, deep-heart encounter with the love of your Heavenly Father. I bless you to encounter His extravagant love in such a tangible way that you will be forever changed, never to be the same again. You're blessed in the Name of the Lord.

Bonus Section

Find More Here

A. Sexuality Reset Prayers[65]

Prayer for Sexual Wholeness: Generational and Personal

Heavenly Father, on behalf of my generations, I acknowledge, confess and repent for choices and actions that brought sexual brokenness into our family line. I ask for your forgiveness and for the blood of the cross of Jesus to be applied to all our sexual sins.

I also repent for my own ungodly sexual choices and actions and turn entirely away from them. Where I've been affected by nurturing and emotional deficiencies from the womb and in childhood, I ask for your balm of love to fill up, heal, and restore every empty, broken, and wounded place in me. I pray for complete separation from all generational patterns of sexual brokenness, all the way back to the time of my conception.

I choose to forgive myself for seeking to fulfill my unmet needs and sexual urges in ways that aren't pleasing to you. I now set my heart to follow your ways.

I also ask that my future children and the generations to come will be completely released from cycles of sexual brokenness. I ask you, Heavenly Father, to establish your righteous ways in our hearts so that we will be free to choose sexual wholeness. In the Name of Jesus I pray. Amen.

Reset Prayer for Sexual False Starts

I choose to believe in my heart that through His blood on the cross, Jesus has paid in full to reset my sexuality back to God's original intent. I anchor my faith on what the Word of God says in Colossians 1:20: "And by the blood of his cross, everything in heaven and earth is brought back to himself—back to its original intent, restored to innocence again!"

I ask for and receive forgiveness for sexual choices and actions against God, myself, and others. I open my life to the cleansing power of the blood of Jesus that makes me whole. Let my heart, thoughts, imagination, emotions, and body be thoroughly cleansed by the blood of Jesus.

Where sexual choices and actions have established neurological, spiritual, and emotional attachments with others, I ask for these unhealthy bonds to be broken in the Name of Jesus. I also ask that where fragments of my soul and the soul of others have been disconnected that they now be returned to their rightful place in each of us. Thank you, Heavenly Father, for restoring and reintegrating our souls to function as you intended.

Through the blood of Jesus and the power of the Holy Spirit, I now receive freedom and protection from any ungodly spiritual forces that may seek to take advantage of the false starts I've had.

As your grace is poured into my heart day by day, empower me to turn entirely away from the path of sexual brokenness. I come into full agreement with your original design of sex for marriage, and my body as a majestic place for your Holy Spirit to live. In the Name of Jesus. Amen.

Reset Prayer for Sexual Abuse

(See "What If You Need a Reset Because of What Someone Did?" in Chapter 10. You may also adapt and pray the Reset Prayer for Sexual False Starts).

Heavenly Father, I receive your supernatural strength and choose to forgive __________ (insert names) for the pain they've caused me. I now receive from you the full reset of my sexuality in the places that were broken by their abuse. I receive your complete cleansing by the blood of Jesus. Thank you for my total freedom from every lingering trace of pain, guilt, shame, loss, and trauma. Restore your peace and wholeness where there has been turmoil in my sexuality. I pray this in the mighty Name of Jesus. Amen.

Abortion: Prayer of Repentance for Mercy, Forgiveness, and Healing

Heavenly Father, I come to you seeking your forgiveness and healing from the abortion I had. I acknowledge that you are the Creator of life, and that I've sinned against you in choosing to end the life of the child I conceived. I'm sorry for also sinning against myself and the child. Your Word promises that if I confess my sins to you, you're faithful to forgive me every time and to cleanse me from all unrighteousness.

Please be merciful to me. Grant me your forgiveness and the power to forgive myself. I know that on the cross Jesus gave His life and paid for all my sins with His blood. I'm grateful that Jesus took my place so that I can have the hope of being restored and healed from this brokenness.

I now receive the blood of Jesus into the depths of my spirit, heart, soul, and body to free me from every grief, pain, shame, and guilt. I receive the purging of my conscience and freedom from every haunting memory.

By faith I step onto the trading floor of your Grace Exchange[66] for a complete reversal of the agreement (trade) I made with death through this abortion. I'm trading my brokenness for your wholeness, and my weaknesses for your strength. In this great exchange, I receive the abundant life that Jesus gives.

In your unfailing mercy and love, I ask you to reset all aspects of my life and give me a new start. I know you did this for others. You did it for King David, who had committed adultery and murder, for Rahab the prostitute who was completely restored and included in the genealogy of Jesus, and for the woman caught in the act of adultery.[67] Thank you for doing it for me too.

Thank you for restoring me to sexual wholeness, for resetting my sexuality, and for giving me a clean, pure heart to honour you. I pray this in the Name of Jesus. Amen.

Psalm 25:6–7, TPT

Forgive my failures as a young man [woman] and overlook the sins of my immaturity. Give me grace, Yahweh! Always look at me through your eyes of love— your forgiving eyes of mercy and compassion. When you think of me, see me as one you love and care for.

Prayer for the Touch of the Master's Hand

(See "The Old Violin" poem in Chapter 10).

Lord Jesus, I acknowledge you as the Master Creator of all things.

By faith I put my broken sexuality into your hands. It has been battered and scarred like the old violin that was being auctioned cheaply. But I believe that with just one touch from your hands that were nailed to Calvary's cross for me, I too can be whole again.

I receive your touch in my spirit, soul, and body for renewed sexual wholeness as you intended for me in the beginning.

I now dedicate my life into your hands and choose to honour you with my sexuality and all that I am. Amen.

B. Reboot Your Mind Collection

Chapter 1: Timing Is Everything

I can do everything through Christ, who gives me strength! (Philippians 4:13, NLT)

But those who wait on the Lord shall renew their strength; they shall mount up with wings like eagles, they shall run and not be weary, they shall walk and not faint. (Isaiah 40:31)

You will keep in perfect peace all who trust in you, all whose thoughts are fixed on you! (Isaiah 26:3, NLT)

"Relationships are most fulfilled when we follow the advice 'not to awaken love until the time is right.'" (Pam Stenzel, Song of Solomon 8:4, NLT)

Chapter 2: Waiting Is for Preparation

"It's better to look ahead and prepare than to look back and regret." (Jackie Joyner-Kersee)

And let us run with perseverance the race marked out for us, fixing our eyes on Jesus, the pioneer and perfecter of faith. For the joy set before him he endured the cross ... (Hebrews 12:1–2)

An athlete who refuses to play by the rules will never get anywhere. (2 Timothy 2:5, The Message)

Chapter 3: It's Worth the Wait

A person without self-control is like a city with broken-down walls. (Proverbs 25:28, NLT)

But the Holy Spirit produces this kind of fruit in our lives ... self-control. (Galatians 5:22, NLT)

"Self-control is not the ability to say no to a thousand other voices. It is the ability to say yes to the one thing so completely that there's nothing left to give to the other options." (Bill Johnson)

#ControlMeself. (Cookie Monster)

Chapter 4: Airplanes and Kisses

Humanly speaking, no one can understand the mysteries of God without the Holy Spirit. (1 Corinthians 2:16, TPT footnote)

Trust in the Lord completely, and do not rely on your own opinions. (Proverbs 3:5a, TPT)

Our Father, dwelling in the heavenly realms ... Forgive us the wrongs we have done as we ourselves release forgiveness to those who have wronged us. (Matthew 6:9a, 12, TPT)

Chapter 5: God's Big Ideas

"Our bodies are not only biological, they are theological—they tell a divine story." (Christopher West)

There's more to sex than mere skin on skin. Sex is as much a spiritual mystery as physical fact. (1 Corinthians 6:16, The Message)

Or didn't you realize that your body is a sacred place, the place of the Holy Spirit? Don't you see that you can't live however you please, squandering what God paid such a high price for? The physical part of you is not some piece of property belonging to the spiritual part of you. God owns the whole works. So let people see God in and through your body. (1 Corinthians 6:19–20, The Message)

Chapter 6: Big Ideas about Relationship

But God demonstrates his own love for us in this: While we were still sinners, Christ died for us. (Romans 5:8, NIV)

"Because of the forgiving power of Christ, you are a new creation no matter what you've done or where you are." (Jim Burns)

And by the blood of his cross, everything in heaven and earth is brought back to himself—back to its original intent, restored to innocence again! (Colossians 1:20, TPT)

Chapter 7: Pursuing Sexual Wholeness

Above all else, guard your heart, for everything you do flows from it. (Proverbs 4:23, NIV)

Trust in the Lord completely, and do not rely on your own opinions. With all your heart rely on him to guide you, and he will lead you in every decision. (Proverbs 3:5, TPT)

"Purity of life is not a quest for perfection as much as it's a quest for liberation from those things that may inhibit effectiveness and reduce power-filled living." (Jack Hayford)

"There is no greater privilege than being a host to God Himself." (Bill & Beni Johnson)

Chapter 8: You're in a Battle

Create a new, clean heart within me. Fill me with pure thoughts and holy desires, ready to please you. (Psalm 51:10, TPT)

"Every battle is won or lost in the arena of your mind." (Cindy Trimm)

"When you change your thoughts, you will change your feelings as well, and you will also eliminate the triggers that set off those feelings." (Michele Goldstein)

Chapter 9: False Starts Are Costly

The thief's purpose is to steal and kill and destroy. My purpose is to give them a rich and satisfying life. (John 10:10, NLT)

Run from sexual sin! No other sin so clearly affects the body as this one does. For sexual immorality is a sin against your own body. (1 Corinthians 6:18, NLT)

I have chosen to be faithful; I have determined to live by your regulations. (Psalm 119:30, NLT)

Chapter 10: Reset Is Possible

But if we own up to our sins, God shows that He is faithful and just by forgiving us of our sins and purifying us from the pollution of all the bad things we have done. (1 John 1:9, The Voice)

"If you have given your virginity away, it is not too late to start over. You cannot get your virginity back, but God can give you a fresh start." (*Why Wait?* Rose Publishing)

So lift your hands and give thanks to God for his marvelous kindness and for his miracles of mercy for those he loves! (Psalm 107:35, TPT)

Chapter 11: You Have a Way of Escape

"The problem is, when we are faced with temptation, we aren't looking for the escape. Maybe we enjoy our secret sin too much, and we don't truly want God's help." (Mary Fairchild)

Wisdom is so priceless that it exceeds the value of any jewel. Nothing you could wish for can equal her. (Proverbs 8:11, TPT)

Don't you know that flirting with the world's values places you at odds with God? Whoever chooses to be the world's friend makes himself God's enemy. (James 4:4b, TPT)

Rather, clothe yourself with the Lord Jesus Christ, and do not think about how to gratify the desires of the flesh, (Romans 13:14, NIV)

Chapter 12: Five Practical Ps for Sexual Wholeness

"Surround yourself with only people who are going to lift you higher." (Oprah Winfrey)

"Sometimes when we think we are strong enough we don't take the necessary steps to protect ourselves from falling into temptation." (Pam Stenzel)

Two are better than one because a good return comes when two work together. If one of them falls, the other can help him up. But who will help the pitiful person who falls down alone? (Ecclesiastes 4:9–10, The Voice)

Chapter 13: Protect What You Love

"When the purpose of a thing is not known, abuse is inevitable." (Dr. Myles Munroe)

There is a sense in which sexual sins are different from all others. In sexual sin we violate the sacredness of our own bodies, these bodies that were made for God-given and God-modeled love, for "becoming one" with another. (1 Corinthians 6:18, The Message)

Chapter 14: See Your Future Now

"You must get an image of what you want to be on the inside first, if you want to see it come to pass in your life on the outside." (Joel Osteen)

"You make sexual choices not based on how you are feeling, but by who you have chosen to become." (Julie Slattery)

If people can't see what God is doing, they stumble all over themselves; But when they attend to what he reveals, they are blessed. (Proverbs 29:18, The Message)

Your word is a lamp to guide my feet and a light for my path. (Psalm 119:105, NLT)

Chapter 15: Never Forget This One Thing

So above all else, let love be the beautiful prize for which you run. (1 Corinthians 13:13b, TPT)

For it is Christ's love that fuels our passion and motivates us, because we are absolutely convinced that he has given his life for all of us. (2 Corinthians 5:14, TPT)

My child, if you truly want a long and satisfying life, never forget the things that I've taught you. Follow closely every truth that I've given you. Then you will have a full, rewarding life. Hold on to loyal love and don't let go, and be faithful to all that you've been taught. Let your life be shaped by integrity, with truth written upon your heart. (Proverbs 3:1–3, TPT)

C. The Father's Blessing

Receive this blessing that your Heavenly Father releases from His heart to yours.

My beloved teen, you are valuable and precious in My sight. I've chosen you in love, and nothing in the universe can separate you from My endless love for you. I've stamped you with my image, so you must know that you are My beloved with whom I am well pleased.

My beloved **son**, I call you an honourable and mighty man of valour.

My beloved **daughter**, I call you a noble woman, lovely and highly favoured in My sight.

May you embrace My unfailing, unconditional love for you and draw from it as the main source of whatever you need. Have no fear of the future, for you can do all things through Christ who strengthens you.

I bless you to receive, carry, and release My presence into the world around you.

D. Teen Life-Stage Blessing

The following blessing is adapted from the author's book, **Recover Your Blessing Birthright**. *It answers the teenage life question, "Do I have what it takes to make it in this world?" This blessing also imparts the patience and self-control that comes from the Holy Spirit.*

***

Beloved teen, may you confidently trust your Heavenly Father to guide your transition from childhood into a season of apprenticeship for adulthood. We, the older generation, bless your rite of passage with heaven's provision for every need. As it was said of Jesus, may you increase in wisdom, in maturity, and in favour with God and people around you!

We bless you to believe with all your heart that there's greatness in you, that God has designed you with everything you need to fulfill His desired purpose and to handle the greater responsibilities of life. By God's grace, you have what it takes to experience wholeness in your sexuality and to excel in all aspects of life. We bless you with divine empowerment and favour to overcome every barrier to your success.

May you surrender any belief or mindset that is motivated by the spirit of the world. Your self-evaluation isn't based on the world's standards but on the unfailing love of your Heavenly Father, who used His divine power to put you together.

With this blessing, we apply the blood of Jesus to your life to free you from unhealthy behaviours, choices, and experiences. In particular, we hold the blood of Jesus on your brain for the rooting out of harmful memories and responses. May you experience ongoing supernatural renewal and growth in your brain for wise decisions.

We bless you with God-appointed mentoring relationships, especially a deepening relationship with the Holy Spirit as your Teacher. May the

Holy Spirit guide you into all truth. You shall be taught by the Lord and great shall be your peace.

For your teenage journey and beyond, we also release into your heart the Spirit of patience and self-control to free you from impulsiveness and to synchronize all aspects of your life with heaven's perfect timing. You're blessed in the Name of the Lord.

E. Bite-Size Blessing Selections

Perfect Love I bless you with the understanding that unlike what's displayed in media and elsewhere, the love of your Heavenly Father is unconditional, unchanging, and always seeks what is best for you. May you settle it in your heart that you are God's beloved, chosen in love, by love and for love. I bless you to enjoy your Father's perfect love and acceptance, and to grow in your love for Him. In turn, may you also love yourself and others as God intends.

And now, may the Lord bless you and protect you. May He smile on you and be gracious to you, show you favour and give you peace. You're blessed in the Name of the Lord.

Chosen I bless you to embrace the truth that you exist because your Heavenly Father chose for you to be on the earth at this time. May you settle it once and for all that you're not here by accident. You're not a mistake. I bless you instead to believe with all your heart that God, your Heavenly Father, planned your arrival with purpose, care, and love. May you cherish the joy of knowing that you were conceived in your mother's womb because God first chose you.

And now, may the Lord bless you and protect you. May He smile on you and be gracious to you, show you favour and give you peace. You're blessed in the Name of the Lord.

Self-Image

I bless you with the ability to develop thoughts and feelings about yourself that are grounded in truth. Above all, the truth that you share God's majestic image because you came from Him. I bless you with complete freedom from any beliefs and experiences that may have created wrong impressions about yourself. May the mental pictures you carry around be imprinted only with the words of your Heavenly Father—words such as loved, appreciated, chosen, royal, honourable, special, masterpiece, great, and valuable.

And now, may the Lord bless you and protect you. May He smile on you and be gracious to you, show you favour and give you peace. You're blessed in the Name of the Lord.

Personal Identity

I bless you with courage to celebrate your one-of-a-kind personal identity. Also with the power to live free from comparison, competition, approval-seeking, and confusion about who God made you to be. May you find joy in knowing that in the eyes of your Heavenly Father, you're His masterpiece, wonderfully designed to display Him to others. I bless you with great success in becoming uniquely you—the person God had in mind when He created you.

And now, may the Lord bless you and protect you. May He smile on you and be gracious to you, show you favour and give you peace. You're blessed in the Name of the Lord.

Spiritual Identity

I bless you with heightened awareness that the core of who you are is spiritual, because God is Spirit and He created you to reflect Him, as a mirror does. So may you place high value on who you are—a spiritual being with a soul in a body. I bless you with courage to use your body for the noble purpose of being a dwelling for God. I bless you to grow and be strengthened with great might from the inside out.

And now, may the Lord bless you and protect you. May He smile on you and be gracious to you, show you favour and give you peace. You're blessed in the Name of the Lord.

Male Sexual Identity

I bless you with divine power to understand deep in your heart that your **male** sexual identity is a gift from your Heavenly Father. On your journey into **manhood**, may you courageously embrace the changes in your body, knowing that they're part of God's design. As you grow, I bless you with an abundance of God's enabling power to protect your thoughts, feelings, emotions, relationships, and choices.

And now, may the Lord bless you and protect you. May He smile on you and be gracious to you, show you favour and give you peace. You're blessed in the Name of the Lord.

Female Sexual Identity

I bless you with divine power to understand deep in your heart that your **female** sexual identity is a gift from your Heavenly Father. On your journey into **womanhood**, may you courageously embrace the changes in your body, knowing that they're part of God's design. As you grow, I bless you with an abundance of God's enabling power to protect your thoughts, feelings, emotions, relationships, and choices.

And now, may the Lord bless you and protect you. May He smile on you and be gracious to you, show you favour and give you peace. You're blessed in the Name of the Lord.

Reset

I bless you with divine power to reset your sexuality by humbly acknowledging to your Heavenly Father when you engage in behaviours that are contrary to His intent. May you trust His heart of mercy for you, receive His forgiveness, and embrace His grace for a fresh start. I bless you with freedom from any associated guilt or shame. May you be wise in seeking the support of others to whom you can be accountable.

And now, may the Lord bless you and protect you. May He smile on you and be gracious to you, show you favour and give you peace. You're blessed in the Name of the Lord.

For the complete collection of Power Edition Bite-Size Blessing please visit https://realidteaching.org/blessing-solutions/

About the Author

Marva M. Tyndale is passionate about the spiritual wellbeing of the next generation and leads a not-for-profit organization (www.realidteaching.org).

She has authored three other books to advance her mission as a messenger of hope to the generations: *Keeping Our Hope Alive* (2008), *911Hope* (2014), and *Recover Your Blessing Birthright* (2018). Marva's essay, "The Mystery of the Creative Impulse," also won the Canadian Authors Association 7th Winners' Circle International Contest (1999). She holds two theological Master's degrees and an honorary Doctor of Divinity.

Marva has four adult children. She is a grandmother and lives in Mississauga, Ontario, Canada with her spouse, Maurice.

Bibliography

Burns, Jim. 2008. *The Purity Code: God's Plan for Sex and Your Body.* Bloomington: Bethany House Publishers.

Covey, Franklin. FranklinCovey Courses: The 7 Habits of Highly Effective People®. "Habit 2: Begin With the End in Mind®". https://www.franklincovey.com/habit-2/#:~:text=Habit%202%3A%20Begin%20With%20the%20End%20in%20Mind%20is%20based,all%20things%20are%20created%20twice.

Covey, Stephen R. 2004. *The 7 Habits of Highly Effective People: Powerful Lessons in Personal Change.* New York, Simon and Schuster.

Evert, Jason and Crystalina Evert and Brian Butler. 2006. *Theology of the Body for Teens: Discovering God's Plan for Love and Life. High School Edition. Student Workbook.* West Chester: Ascension Press.

Evert, Jason. 2008. *Theology of the Body for Teens: Discovering God's Plan for Love and Life. High School Edition. Parent's Guide.* West Chester: Ascension Press.

Flood San Diego Church. *The Marshmallow Experiment—Instant Gratification.* YouTube Video, 4:42. Posted by "FloodSanDiego." April 29, 2010. https://www.youtube.com/watch?v=Y04WF3cSd9Q.

Johns Hopkins Medicine. Health Conditions and Diseases. "Brain Anatomy and How the Brain Works." https://www.hopkinsmedicine.org/health/conditions-and-diseases/

anatomy-of-the-brain#:~:text=The%20brain%20is%20a%20complex,central%20nervous%20system%2C%20or%20CNS.

McCullen, Aidan. "Where there is no vision, the people perish." *The Thursday Thought Medium* (blog). March 15, 2018. https://aidanmccullen.com/where-there-is-no-vision-the-people-perish/.

McDowell, Josh and Day, Dick. 1987. *Why Wait: What You Need to Know about the Teen Sexuality Crisis.* Nashville: Thomas Nelson Publishers

NeuroscienceNews. The Conversation. "Watching pornography rewires the brain to a more juvenile state." December 29, 2019. https://neurosciencenews.com/neuroscience-pornography-brain-15354/#:~:text=Porn%20scenes%2C%20like%20addictive%20substances,to%20natural%20sources%20of%20pleasure.

PBS. *Resisting the marshmallow and the success of self control.* YouTube Video, 9:21. Posted by "PBS NewsHour." January 8, 2015. https://www.youtube.com/watch?v=BLtQaRrDsC4

Pearcey, Nancy R. 2018. *Love Thy Body: Answering Hard Questions about Life and Sexuality.* Grand Rapids: Baker Books.

Rose Publishing. 2000. *Why Wait? 24 Reasons to Wait Until Marriage to Have Sex.* Torrence: RW Research Inc.

Sesame Workshop. *Sesame Street: Me Want It (But Me Wait).* YouTube Video, 3:10. Posted by "Sesame Street." August 5, 2013. https://www.youtube.com/watch?v=9PnbKL3wuH4.

Slattery, Juli. 2017. *Sex and the Single Girl.* Chicago: Moody Press.

Stensel, Pam and Melissa Nesdahl. 2010. *Nobody Told Me: What You Need to Know About the Physical and Emotional Consequences of Sex Outside of Marriage.* Ventura: Regal From Gospel Light.

TallyPress. "Five Rules Your Probably Didn't Know About the 100m Sprint." https://tallypress.com/fun/5-rules-you-probably-didnt-know-about-the-100m-sprint/.

Tyndale, Marva M. 2018. *Recover Your Blessing Birthright: Transforming Lives and Culture with the Gift of Words.* Ontario: Summerhill Publishing.

University of Rochester Medical Center. Health Encyclopedia. "Understanding the Teen Brain." https://www.urmc.rochester.edu/encyclopedia/content.aspx?ContentTypeID=1&ContentID=3051.

West, Christopher. 2009. *Theology of the Body for Beginners: A Basic Introduction to Blessed John Paul II's Sexual Revolution.* West Chester: Ascension Press.

END NOTES

Chapter 1

1 TallyPress, “Five Rules Your Probably Didn’t Know about the 100m Sprint,” August 6, 2016, https://tallypress.com/fun/5-rules-you-probably-didnt-know-about-the-100m-sprint/.

2 Mark 9:23, NLT.

3 Psalm 27:14, TPT.

Chapter 2

4 Wikipedia, “Jackie Joyner-Kersee,” accessed July 19, 2020, https://en.wikipedia.org/wiki/Jackie_Joyner-Kersee.

5 BrainyQuote, “Jackie Joyner-Kersee Quotes,” accessed July 19, 2020, https://www.brainyquote.com/authors/jackie-joyner-kersee-quotes.

6 See Hebrews 12:1–2.

7 See the “Reboot Your Mind” Collection in the Bonus Section.

Chapter 3

8 Flood San Diego Church, The Marshmallow Experiment—Instant Gratification, YouTube Video, 4:42, posted by “FloodSanDiego,” April 29, 2010, https://www.youtube.com/watch?v=Y04WF3cSd9Q.

9 PBS, Resisting the marshmallow and the success of self control, YouTube Video, 9:21, posted by “PBS NewsHour,” January 8, 2015, https://www.youtube.com/watch?v=BLtQaRrDsC4.

10 Sesame Workshop, Sesame Street: Me Want It (But Me Wait), YouTube Video, 3:10, posted by “Sesame Street,” August 5, 2013, https://www.youtube.com/watch?v=9PnbKL3wuH4.

11 Marva Tyndale, Timing—Power Blessing Edition Day 15, YouTube Video, 1:19, posted by “bite-size blessing,” November 23, 2020, https://www.youtube.com/watch?v=_Huij2z_z3U.

Chapter 5

12 1 Thessalonians 5:23.

Chapter 6

13 Luke 3:38; Genesis 1:28–30, 2:15–25, 3:8.

14 Revelation 19:7.

15 Genesis 3:7–8.

16 1 Peter 1:19–20; Revelation 13:8.

17 2 Corinthians 5:17.

Chapter 7

18 Matthew 19:8, The Voice.

19 University of Rochester Medical Center, Health Encyclopedia, "Understanding the Teen Brain," accessed April 26, 2022, https://www.urmc.rochester.edu/encyclopedia/content.aspx?ContentTypeID=1&ContentID=3051.

20 Daniel 1:8.

21 Luke 1:35, NLT.

22 Isaiah 7:14, NLT.

23 Psalm 32:8, NLT.

Chapter 8

24 Christopher West, Theology of the Body for Beginners: A Basic Introduction to Blessed John Paul II's Sexual Revolution (West Chester: Ascension Press, 2009), 11.

25 Proverbs 4:23, NLT.

26 Mark 7:21, NIV.

27 James 4:8b, The Voice.

Chapter 9

28 1 Corinthians 6:16, The Message.

29 Johns Hopkins Medicine, Health Conditions and Diseases, "Brain Anatomy and How the Brain Works, accessed April 26, 2022, https://www.hopkinsmedicine.org/health/conditions-and-diseases/

anatomy-of-the-brain#:~:text=The%20brain%20is%20a%20complex,central%20nervous%20system%2C%20or%20CNS.

30 NeuroscienceNews, The Conversation, "Watching pornography rewires the brain to a more juvenile state," December 29, 2019, https://neurosciencenews.com/neuroscience-pornography-brain-15354/#:~:text=Porn%20scenes%2C%20like%20addictive%20substances,to%20natural%20sources%20of%20pleasure.

31 Ephesians 2:10, NLT.

32 Ecclesiastes 3:11.

Chapter 10

33 Hebrews 4:16.

34 John 1:14.

35 Romans 5:17, 6:14.

36 Genesis 38:1–30; Joshua 2:1–21, 6:22–25; 2 Samuel 11:1–5, 12:24–25; Ruth 4:1-6; Matthew 1:3, 5, 6.

37 Romans 5:1-9; Titus 3:7.

38 Jim Burns, The Purity Code: God's Plan for Sex and Your Body (Bloomington: Bethany House Publishers, 2008), 162.

39 Genesis 41:50–52, 48:20.

40 Myra Brooks Welch, OnlyTheBible, "The Old Violin: The Touch of the Master's Hand," last modified April 30, 2010, https://www.onlythebible.com/Poems/the-Touch-of-the-Masters-Hand--Old-Violin.html.

Chapter 11

41 Hebrews 4:15.

42 Romans 13:14.

43 1 Corinthians 1:30.

44 Youth Unlimited, Young Life, Global 180, and Power to Change are excellent resource in Canada that you may be able to connect with by searching online for locations near you.

45 Revelation 12:11, NLT.

46 Zechariah 4:6, The Voice.

Chapter 12

47 Matthew 6:33.

48 Proverbs 1:10.

49 Psalm 119:37, 101:3; Matthew 6:22–23.

50 Psalm 103:20.

51 1 John 1:9.

52 Proverbs 24:16, NLT.

53 James 4:6.

Chapter 14

54 Franklin Covey, Courses: The 7 Habits of Highly Effective People®, "Habit 2: Begin With the End in Mind®", https://www.franklincovey.com/habit-2/#:~:text=Habit%202%3A%20Begin%20With%20the%20End%20in%20Mind%20is%20based,all%20things%20are%20created%20twice.

55 Proverbs 29:18, KJV.

56 Aidan McCullen, "Where there is no vision, the people perish," The Thursday Thought Medium (blog), March 15, 2018, https://aidanmccullen.com/where-there-is-no-vision-the-people-perish/.

57 Habakkuk 2:2.

58 Habakkuk 2:2-3, The Message.

59 Ecclesiastes 3:11.

Chapter 15

60 See Hebrews 10:5.

61 Luke 1:35; Matthew 1:18.

62 Matthew 3:17.

63 Matthew 4:3, NLT.

64 John 14:9, NLT.

Bonus Section

65 See 1 John 1:8–9; John 10:10; Colossians 1:20 TPT; Psalm 23:3, 30:2, 147:3; Ephesians 1:7.

66 See Chapter 10.

67 See Psalm 51:1–11; Joshua 2:1–21; Matthew 1:5; John 8:1–11.

Any man (boy) who wants your body before you are MARRIED is only out to please himself! He doesn't really give a hoot about you! Once he's had YOU, he's onto the next!! AVOID this guy as you would a rattle snake. An excellent scripture is "I can do all things through Jesus who is my strength." Jesus wants PURITY for you!! Once you give your purity away, you can NEVER NEVER get it back. Again. GUARD YOUR HEART!

CPSIA information can be obtained
at www.ICGtesting.com
Printed in the USA
BVHW091018061122
651205BV00005B/16

9 781039 144224